101 Organic GARDENING HACKS

Eco-friendly Solutions to Improve any Garden

Shawna Coronado

COOL SPRINGS PRESS
Home and Garden Experts™

MINNEAPOLIS, MINNESOTA

Quarto is the authority on a wide range of topics.

Quarto educates, entertains and enriches the lives of our readers—enthusiasts and lovers of hands-on living.

www.quartoknows.com

First published in 2017 by Cool Springs Press,
an imprint of Quarto Publishing Group USA Inc.,
400 First Avenue North, Suite 400, Minneapolis, MN 55401 USA.
Telephone: (612) 344-8100 Fax: (612) 344-8692

quartoknows.com
Visit our blogs at quartoknows.com

Cool Springs Press titles are also available at discounts in bulk quantity for industrial or sales-promotional use. For details contact the Special Sales Manager at Quarto Publishing Group USA Inc., 400 First Avenue North,Suite 400, Minneapolis, MN 55401 USA.

10 9 8 7 6 5 4 3 2

ISBN: 978-1-59186-662-6

Library of Congress Cataloging-in-Publication Data
Names: Coronado, Shawna, author.
Title: 101 organic gardening hacks : eco-friendly solutions to
    improve any garden / Shawna Coronado.
Other titles: One hundred one organic gardening hacks
Description: Minneapolis, MN : Cool Springs Press, 2017. | Includes index.
Identifiers: LCCN 2016022256 | ISBN 9781591866626 (sc)
Subjects: LCSH: Organic gardening.
Classification: LCC SB453.5 .C66 2017 | DDC 635/.0484--dc23
LC record available at https://lccn.loc.gov/2016022256

Acquiring Editor: Mark Johanson
Project Manager: Alyssa Bluhm
Art Director: Cindy Samargia Laun
Cover Design and Illustrations: Jessie Schneider
Book Design and Layout: Diana Boger

Printed in China

> Garden hacking a gorgeous outdoor room, filled with recycled materials, resale shop finds, and reused items for little to no cost, is easy. It is all about the very sustainable process of searching your community for treasures and keeping those items out of the landfill by reusing them smartly.

CONTENTS

INTRODUCTION

HACKING IS THE concept of breaking traditional rules to discover a creative way to accomplish something—a clever trick that saves cash for the thrifty or solves a problem elegantly. Whether the hack is for gardening, computing, cooking, or anything in between, "hacking" your way through your daily challenges is fast becoming a new lifestyle choice because the best hacks are easy, smart, and economical.

My garden has always been a hotbed for green and organic garden hacks (although I didn't always call them that). With a limited budget, I am constantly on the lookout for alternative ways to build a useful, beautiful, low-cost,

∧ Standing in my front lawn organic vegetable garden, I realized the potential of the garden for both my neighborhood and myself—an environmentally friendly garden can truly make a difference for you as an individual and for the community at large.

and low-input garden. Throw in a bit of creativity and art, and you have an environmentally responsible, delightfully whimsical, yet eminently practical garden that enhances your home's value and brings joy to the neighbors.

People often ask me where I get my ideas. Without a doubt, my grandmothers were—and continue to be—my greatest inspiration. They were queens of the garden hack; reusing old nylon pantyhose to tie tomatoes to stakes, using rotted sheep manure to fertilize, and using recycled tuna cans to deter cutworms, they showed me that having a healthy, organic, environmentally friendly garden is possible, and with very little financial investment. Soil, seeds, sunshine, and hard work can outwit just about any life challenge, according to my grandmothers.

One thing you learn from grandparents who grew up in a wartime era—they wasted nothing, and they saved everything. The folks of their generation were the ultimate reducers, reusers, and recyclers.

Globally, humans generate 2.6 trillion pounds of garbage annually. Almost half of that waste comes from organic matter, such as food. This resource could easily be turned into billions of pounds of compost to use in food and agricultural growing, yet it is discarded.

When we use creative and environmentally friendly garden hacks, we are helping the environment by keeping items out of the landfill for longer. But more importantly, by converting waste products into useful goods, you can grow a healthy garden at no-to-low cost. Ultimately, garden hacks are about wellness: an overall state of well-being not just for you, but for the entire planet.

^ Upcycling wine bottles, old tools, and old stone into a creative and beautiful path for a dark area on the side of your home is the ultimate green garden hack. Plant herbs and vegetables in the wall garden, and you have the opportunity to grow organic food for your family.

Making your own compost or garden soil is a classic garden hack that helps you grow your own organic herbs, vegetables, and fruit—and in the process, helps you feed your family with fresh, chemical-free food.

The statistics vary on municipal solid waste disposal. Globally, food is half the waste thrown in landfills. In the United States, however, food combined with yard trimmings and paper is more than half of what is thrown in the garbage. If we used yard trimmings and brush to make healthy, organic compost, we could prevent millions of tons of garbage. Paper and cardboard can be reused in the garden in dozens of ways because they compost as well. As newspapers are now printed with soy ink, which is safe for the environment, it makes sense to reuse as much of it as possible in your garden hack adventures.

In my front garden, I have built a place that can be loved and appreciated by hummingbirds, pollinators, and neighbors alike thanks to garden hacks. By building a rainwater cistern to collect free water, using organic fertilizers, planting a garden filled with pollinator-attracting plants, and utilizing soils I have made myself, I am practicing sustainable growing ideas, which help both my family and the community stay a little greener and healthier.

While saving money is very important to gardeners, there is also a byproduct of using good environmental practices in building a beautiful garden: friendship.

∧ I have done everything I can to make my front garden visually interesting, as well as natural and environmentally friendly. For example, my water fountain is made from 100-percent post-consumer recycled products: it's actually a 500-gallon cistern that collects rainwater off my roof as its water source.

< Keeping an item out of the landfill is especially rewarding when you translate it into an artful garden hack.

Community is about caring, and there's no better garden hack than splitting a pass-along plant to share with a neighbor, or sharing the bounty of all those extra vegetables you grew from seed to help build the bond of companionship with your friends. By taking the step to be a little greener and healthier, you set an example for others in your community to help teach organic stewardship. Neighborhoods the world over are primed and ready for garden hack love, because when you build something out of love, others want to share in that experience.

The garden hacks you'll discover in my book range from soil creation and upcycled outdoor living ideas to pest management and quick tips on starting seeds—all as natural as I could make them. Many of the hacks are based on what my lovely money-saving grandmothers taught me while I was growing up on the farm in Indiana. Making a difference with your family's environmentally friendly lifestyle is the first small step to making a difference for a better world. Start building greener and healthier gardens today.

> Butterflies love native plants such as butterfly weed and black-eyed Susans, but they also adore annuals such as zinnia. Planting a few big zinnias all around your beds is a wonderfully easy garden hack.

∨ Dwight and Vivian Lund came to my front garden to help me divide some plants to share with the community. Their sage advice and contributions to the garden inspired me to believe that a sustainable and environmentally friendly garden can be a part of a sharing community.

DIRTY, rotten HACKS

HACKS IN THIS CHAPTER

1

RETIRE YOUR TILLER

If you love your soil, stop flipping it over

SOMETIMES THE BEST way to improve something is to let it be. A no-till garden is a perfect example, and creating one also means less work for you.

Imagine building a large garden without having to turn over the soil in your garden beds. Turning soil kills the microbes living beneath the ground that contribute to a healthier root system by living symbiotically with your roots. There are billions of bacteria, millions of fungi, thousands of protozoa, and scores of other nematodes and organisms found in one small tablespoon of healthy soil. Hacking your garden soil with a few simple no-till tips can make for hugely successful growing because you keep those vital creatures alive and happy in your garden beds.

A no-till garden has other benefits. Because you are consistently smothering weeds with mulch or compost, they struggle to grow there. And undisturbed, enriched soil requires far less fertilizer in order to support successful plants. The no-till technique works in almost any garden space and can help grow extremely healthy organic vegetables and herbs.

< This front lawn vegetable garden was grown with the no-till method. Organic fertilizer was placed in the planting holes at the time of planting, but no other fertilizer was added afterward.

∧ Here you see a layer of organic soil being added to the front lawn vegetable garden.

∧ Follow the initial garden planting with regular water and occasional, as-needed weeding.

HOW TO CREATE A NO-TILL GARDEN

Instead of turning of your soil over for a garden, start by removing all the grass either by stripping the sod or smothering the grass (see Hack 80: "Hack Away Unwanted Grass by Smothering It").

1. Put down a 2-inch layer of rotted manure or compost on top of the bare soil. Do not turn the soil over.
2. Dig holes to plant your plants.
3. Mulch the garden the first year with wood chips or another natural mulch, such as pine needles, rotted leaves, or straw.
4. After the harvest at the end of the season, do not pull out the vegetable or herb plants by the root; cut their stems at the base of the soil and leave the roots in the ground to overwinter and eventually rot. Compost the cut plant matter.
5. Next planting year, cover the garden with another 2-inch layer of compost.
6. When planting new vegetables and herbs, only pull out roots from the previous year if they block an area for a new plant. Be sure to rotate the crop so that no plant from the previous season is planted in the same location in the current year.
7. In your third planting year, follow the same practices, but add a layer of mulch instead of a layer of compost.
8. In your fourth planting year, follow the same practices, but add a layer of soil instead of a layer of mulch.
9. In the fifth planting year, follow the same practices, but add a layer of rotted manure instead of a layer of soil.
10. In the sixth planting year, follow the same practices, but add a layer of compost instead of rotted manure.
11. Continue every season layering up the compost, mulch, soil, and rotted manure without ever turning it over.

2

PUT WASTE TO WORK
Composted manure is garden gold

HACKING YOUR OWN garden soil is not as hard as it sounds: all you need is some amazingly rich, composted, all-natural material to toss in your garden beds. Layering the compost and other organic materials eventually transforms your garden soil into a wonderland of healthy microbes that your plants' roots love.

Rotted manure is an excellent addition to your soil. It increases microbes and generally creates a more stable environment for your roots (don't worry, composted manure has no foul smell). The only issue is how to get your hands on some. Try searching for manure at a local horse or cow farm. Always ask how long the manure pile has been sitting—it takes at least six months for weed seeds and pathogens to be killed in a pile that has a core temperature of 140 to 150 degrees Fahrenheit for 30 to 60 days within that time period. Most farmers can give you an accurate estimate on how long the product has been cooking.

If you live in an urban area or cannot locate a farm nearby, packaged manure is easy to find. Most garden centers sell bagged composted manure or a compost-manure mix for a reasonable price. Bagged manure is heated during the composting process, which kills weed seeds and pathogens, while retaining the basic benefits of the amendments.

You should not use raw manure fresh from an animal on your plants because most will burn the plants. Additionally, you should never use manure from meat-eating animals such as dogs or cats on your garden beds because it can increase the risk that your family will consume bad bacteria. Hog manure can contain parasites such as roundworms and other pests. You want to use rotted—or composted—manure from an herbivore source (such as cow, bison, llama, or horse) that has been aged for around six months.

< Rotted manure can be delivered to your urban front drive by a local farmer, or you can source bagged manure at the local garden center.

3

SEEK OUT FREE MULCH
Five sources for gratis groundcover

YOU DON'T NEED to look further than most convenience store parking lots to find poly bags of mulch for sale. But why pay $5 a bag for shredded and dyed mulch when other sources offer a bottomless source of free mulch? Here are five sources for free mulch that you can track down no matter where you live.

WHAT'S SO GREAT ABOUT MULCH?

Natural mulch serves many purposes. It suppresses weeds, retains moisture, cools roots, delivers micronutrients as it decomposes, and keeps the garden bed looking attractive. Mulch your gardens 1 to 3 inches deep; more than 4 inches of mulch can harm some plants. Be sure to mulch trees, shrubs, and plants using a flat donut shape around the stem—do not mulch in a volcano shape as it can promote disease and other problems.

< Many townships and cities provide free wood chips for residents to pick up. Some road crews will deliver the mulch to you in 5-yard increments at no to low cost, or you can pick up chips at a designated location.

- **Leaf mold** If you have trees, you have leaves (and if your neighbor has trees, you probably have their leaves too). Shredded leaves are perhaps the best mulch ever for your garden. In the fall, rake all the leaves on your property into a large pile and water it heavily. If you have warm weather through winter, water the pile occasionally. Once spring arrives, dig down into the pile and discover rotted leaf mold. Spread the rotted leaf mold on your garden beds.
- **Grass clippings** As you mow your yard, gather the grass clippings and place them in a pile at the back of your property. Turn the pile frequently and let it dry out. Once dry, you will have a nitrogen-rich source of mulch.
- **Pine boughs and pine needles** Wait until fall to limb up any pine or evergreen branches, use them for holiday decorations, and then place them on top of the garden beds for the rest of winter. In spring, remove the sticks,

but let the pine needles stay on top of the soil as a mulch. This is a great way to use last year's Christmas tree.
- **Animal manures** Rotted manure (see Hack 2) is highly beneficial for your garden and can often be obtained for free at local farms.
- **Township or city wood chip mulch** Wood chip mulch created by road maintenance crews is available in nearly every city or township for free. For use as mulch, wood chips that have set for a while in a large pile are a better choice than fresh chips. You might see the pile steaming in the early mornings: this is a sign that the wood chip pile, much like compost, has heated up internally. Heat kills fungi and diseases, making the mulch perfectly safe to use in your gardens. If chips are not composted, apply an organic nitrogen fertilizer at a rate of ½ pound per 100 square feet of chips so the garden does not suffer from depleted nitrogen.

4

HACK YOUR WAY THROUGH A DRY SPELL
The secret to retaining water

DROUGHT IS DEVASTATING to a garden, and it seems to be more prevalent with every passing year. With watering restrictions and expensive fines for heavy water use, it truly makes sense to hack the drought so your plants can withstand low-water/high-heat conditions.

Water-retentive soil is the number-one tool for keeping moisture close to plant root systems. One key to water-retentive gardening is to practice a no-till approach (see Hack 1: "Retire Your Tiller"). It also helps to amend beds regularly with rich compost material that absorbs and holds water. Whether for containers or garden beds, create drought-resistant soil with the recipe on the right.

> HOMEMADE WATER-RETENTIVE SOIL MIX HACK
> - 1 part organic potting soil with worm castings
> - 1 part organic rotted composted manure
> - 1 part plain compost

∧ Planting succulents and drought-specific plants in containers is a great way to present a stylish garden with minimal water requirements. *Photo taken by Shawna at P. Allen Smith's Moss Mountain Farm garden; www.pallensmith.com.*

OTHER TIPS FOR IMPROVING WATER RETENTION

- For container gardens, do not use the soil mixes that contain artificial water gels and chemical ingredients. Use a natural water-retentive soil mix instead (see the recipe on page 13).
- Succulents and cactus are strongly drought tolerant but require excellent drainage and a soil made specifically for succulents or cactus (see Hack 5: "Make Your Own Mix: Cactus and Succulents").
- Cover your garden with 1 to 3 inches of mulch. Watering deeply once per week is much more effective than frequent shallow watering. Watering during the height of the day will result in much of the water being lost to evaporation; instead, water with drip systems after 8 p.m. or before 8 a.m. Instead of drip watering daily, experiment with watering for a longer time every four days to conserve water.
- Include succulents, cacti, and drought-tolerant groundcovers in container plantings and ground plantings. They are much better choices than water-sucking plants like grass and delicate annuals. Plant appropriately—sun plants in sun areas and shade plants in shade areas.
- Plant vegetables and herbs with smaller leaves; generally speaking, small-leaved plants lose less moisture due to transpiration.
- Vegetable gardening is possible in drought if you use a combination of retentive soil, mulch, organic fertilizers, and vegetables or herbs that require less water.
- Planting vegetables closer together helps conserve water; each plant can shade and protect the other plants, and they share water this way.
- Vegetables and herbs that tolerate drought include beans and peas bred for the Southwest such as tepary beans, black-eyed peas, pole beans, and lima beans. Other possible vegetables include broccoli, chard, Chinese cabbage, eggplant, lavender, Malabar spinach, okra, oregano, peppers, rosemary, sage, thyme, and winter savory.

5

MAKE YOUR OWN MIX:
CACTUS AND SUCCULENTS

An easy alternative to boutique bagged mixes

SUCCULENTS AND CACTI are very popular plants in gardens all over the world, in part because they can survive in so many different climates. Hacking your own homemade soil for these uniquely beautiful plants is easy to do if you follow the formula below; it may be used for indoor or outdoor containers or in planting beds.

> HOMEMADE CACTUS AND SUCCULENT
> SOIL MIX FORMULA
> - 1 part organic potting soil with worm castings
> - 1 part perlite or pumice
> - 1 part coarse builder's sand

> Build a successful container of succulents or cacti with your own homemade organic cactus or succulent soil mix.

TIP: Wear protective gear with prickly cacti, and use grabbing tools such as tongs wrapped with tape to help protect your hands from the spikes when you plant them. Fertilize with organic cactus or succulent food when planting and again during the spring and summer. Do not fertilize in the winter.

WHAT'S SO GREAT ABOUT SUCCULENTS?

Most succulents, including cacti, are fairly tough and can thrive down to 40°F at night, but they prefer day temperatures that range from 70°F to about 85°F. There are several types of sedums, for instance, that can survive seemingly arctic-like winter conditions in the North. They are grown for their drought-tolerant tendencies, interesting architectural forms, and beautiful range of colors. Cacti and succulents look as marvelous on patios and balconies as they do in the ground.

When planting these drought-tolerant plants, it is important that they receive consistent drainage. If you live in a northern climate, certain varieties of cacti and succulents might die out in the cold winter. Having a plan for what you might do with a cactus or succulent plant in the winter is wise—for example, placing them in portable containers that enable you to move them if needed helps the plant have a longer life. Once planted, keep in mind that although many succulents prefer bright light, they can scorch when placed in hot direct sunlight. When placed in too little light, the plants grow leggy and out of shape in order to access the light.

6

DO YOUR HOMEWORK:
TAKE A FREE PERCOLATION TEST
Find out for yourself if your soil holds water

RUNNING A PERCOLATION test is the best way for you to discover how well your soil absorbs water, which in turn enables you to determine what soil amendments you need for your garden. There are many expensive procedures to help discover the percolation rates for your septic drain field, for example, or for any other larger draining systems. For the average homeowner, however, it is easy to successfully hack your own homemade percolation test.

Knowing how fast water drains from your planting areas is the first step toward correcting any drainage issues that may impact the success of your gardening efforts. Poor drainage holds water in one location, forming a block that prevents air from reaching plant roots. Too much water and not enough air is an unhealthy planting zone for root systems (unless you are planting water-loving plants).

< Dig a hole about 12 inches deep by 12 inches in diameter to begin your percolation test.

HOW TO TEST PERCOLATION

1. Dig a hole about 12 inches deep by 12 inches in diameter (see photo).
2. Fill the hole with a bucket of water that will saturate the soil completely.
3. Now wait for the water to completely drain out of the hole.
4. Repeat the procedure, filling the hole with water again, then letting the water drain completely. Your soil should be very saturated with water at this time.
5. Get a measuring stick you can rest inside the hole, then fill the hole with water a third time.
6. Mark the time at the beginning of the fill and calculate how long it takes for the water to drain out of the hole using the inches on the measuring stick as your measuring guide. Measure every hour.
7. If the water is slow to drain, taking 4 to 10 hours to seep into the soil, you have poorly drained soil and might consider plants that tolerate wet feet. If you want to plant a variety of plants in a poorly draining area, then you will need to install better drainage such as a French drain, then heavily amend the soil with organic or natural soil additions to support better draining, or build a raised planting bed above the poor draining area.
8. An extremely fast percolation rate (when the soil drains within minutes) can indicate that the soil is very sandy or rocky. Your easiest options for dealing with fast-draining soil is to plant things that like those conditions. You can also build raised planting beds for a quick fix. For a more permanent repair, amend the soil with organic or natural soil additions, such as compost, that hold water and slow down drainage rates.
9. Ideal soil drainage—neither too fast nor too slow—averages at about 2 inches per hour, but a rate anywhere between 1 and 3 inches is fine for most garden plants.

7

MAKE YOUR OWN MIX: CONTAINER GARDENS

All-purpose potting soil for multiple uses

GARDEN SUCCESS STARTS with understanding your soil and adding the appropriate soil amendments. Hacking your own potting soil for your container gardening needs makes it easier to create an environment in which roots can get the nutritional material they need. And by making your own, you can save plenty of money and control how much you have on hand (how many half-empty bags of potting soil are in your garden shed right now?).

For containers, a soil that is less airy and a bit heavier will result in better water retention, which aids root systems. This also creates an environment in which you will need to water less frequently and in smaller amounts. You can create this heavier soil yourself or mix a traditional potting soil with other natural ingredients. My favorite container soil additive ingredients include compost and worm castings. If you can't find bagged worm castings, consider making your own in a kitchen worm casting bin. Compost and organic matter can include rotted manure, chopped leaves or leaf mold, and traditional food compost (organic foods create organic compost). Adding compost to containers and in-ground plantings is one of the best ways to encourage microbial growth in order to improve root systems.

Here is a homemade soil mix that is great for planting container gardens as well as a soil additive for in-ground planting. Start with an organic potting soil. Be sure to add a cup or two of the worm castings directly to your soil mix

HOMEMADE CONTAINER PLANTING MIX
• 1 part organic potting soil (with worm castings)
• 1 part organic composted manure
• 1 part compost or leaf mold

∧ Mix the organic ingredients together to hack your own recipe for successful potting soil.

if you are able, or purchase a potting soil that already has worm castings as an ingredient. Mix in rotted composted manure and homemade compost or leaf mold, using a 1:3 mixture.

DO YOUR HOMEWORK: TAKE A NO-COST SOIL pH TEST

Acid or alkali? Find out for free

SOIL pH IS A MEASURE of the acidity or alkalinity of your garden soil. The pH scale ranges from 0.0 to 14.0, with 14.0 being the maximum alkaline level and 0.0 the most acid. A reading of 7.0 is considered neutral, neither acid nor alkaline. Knowing your soil's pH can help you make adjustments that can make a real difference in your garden. Some plants perform better in alkaline soil, some prefer acidic soil, and some plants like a neutral environment. Rather than pay for an expensive mail-away test, it is easy to determine general alkalinity by hacking the test yourself. This will not give you a specific numeric result, but it will help you determine how to amend your soil as needed for your favorite plants.

SUPPLIES NEEDED

- Glass cup
- Distilled water
- White vinegar
- Baking soda
- Spoon for stirring
- Spade for digging

HOW TO IDENTIFY ALKALINE SOIL

1. Dig ¼ cup of soil from the planting area you want to test.
2. Mix with distilled water to make a muddy liquid.
3. Pour ¼ cup of white vinegar over the top of the soil.
4. If the mixture bubbles up, it is alkaline soil.

HOW TO IDENTIFY ACIDIC SOIL

1. Dig ¼ cup of soil from the planting area you want to test.
2. Mix with distilled water to make a muddy liquid.
3. Sprinkle baking soda over the top.
4. If the mixture bubbles up, it is acid soil.

HOW TO CHANGE SOIL pH

In order to correct the soil based on your pH test results, you will need to add organic or natural soil amendments. With a higher level of organic matter in the soil, it will take less work to correct acidity in either direction. Compost and humic material works best.

If you have alkaline soil and would like to make it more acidic, add natural ingredients like rotted manure, rotted leaf mold (especially oak leaf compost), and pine needles.

If you have acid soil and would like to make it more alkaline, follow package directions and add natural ingredients like dolomitic lime (made from lime stone), bonemeal, powdered crab or oyster shells, or sparingly use woodstove ashes.

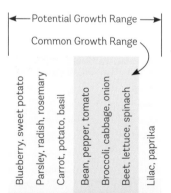

← Potential Growth Range →

Common Growth Range

Blueberry, sweet potato
Parsley, radish, rosemary
Carrot, potato, basil
Bean, pepper, tomato
Broccoli, cabbage, onion
Beet, lettuce, spinach
Lilac, paprika

pH scale

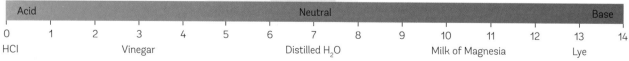

Acid						Neutral						Base	
0	1	2	3	4	5	6	7	8	9	10	11	12	13	14

HCl   Vinegar   Distilled H₂O   Milk of Magnesia   Lye

CONQUER THE ART OF COMPOSTING
Learn the right way to rot

< Whether you live in the country or an urban area, it is possible to tuck a composter behind your home or on a balcony so you can hack natural compost by using food waste.

CONVERTING KITCHEN AND GARDEN waste into usable soil is what composting is all about. Food waste, grass clippings, weeds, small brush, coffee grounds, eggshells—all of these organic ingredients should go into your compost pile, not the landfill. When adding material to the composter, keep in mind the pile needs regular moisture and a proper ratio of carbon-rich materials, or "browns," and nitrogen-rich materials, or "greens" (see Hack 15: "Round Up Your Compost Components: The Browns").

Effective, efficient composting requires active participation on your part. Turn the pile regularly with a garden fork for quicker decomposition. Typically, it takes three to four weeks to create usable compost. If you add "hotter" items, which have a heavier nitrogen content, they can create a heated pile, then the compost can develop more quickly. The speed of compost creation is determined by what you add—maintain a good balance of moisture, carbon, and nitrogen—whether you chop up the ingredients before adding them, and how often you turn the pile.

The temperature of the managed pile is important—it indicates the activity of the decomposition process. It should be warm or hot to the touch. If it is not, then the microbial activity has slowed down, and you need to add more green materials. This heat can be encouraged if you place your compost pile in full sun.

Keeping the pile moist is also important: Organic waste needs water to decompose. Graywater, such as old dishwater or washing machine water, can be drained into a compost pile regularly. The rule of thumb is to keep the pile as moist as a wrung-out sponge. If you actively manage the composting, within a few weeks, you will have a rich additive for your garden.

10

CREATE CUSTOM COMPOST:
LEAF MOLD COMPOST
A favorite of compost connoisseurs

FALL IS THE TIME to get your leaf mold compost going. Considered by many to be one of the richest composts available, leaf mold compost is also 100-percent free, making it is simply a matter of letting your leaves decompose naturally. The process, called cold-composting, is slow because piles of leaves must cure over the winter or even over several seasons.

Leaf mold compost has amazing moisture retaining ability and can hold up to five times its own weight in water. This makes it a marvelous garden bed mulch. Dig leaf mold compost into the soil when planting vegetables or mix it into containers as a way to help heighten moisture retention. Use it anywhere you might use compost or mulch.

THREE VARIATIONS OF LEAF MOLD COMPOST

- **Lazy Gardener Leaf Mold Compost** Rake a large amount of leaves into a big pile, wait two years, and do nothing else. Compost will be rich, brown, and crumbly.

- **Impatient Gardener Leaf Mold Compost** Rake a large amount of leaves together. Use a lawnmower or leaf shredder to chop up the leaves. Pile the shredded leaves in a quiet spot in the shade and keep the pile moist. Turn the pile several times over winter if you are able. In the early summer—about 8 to 12 months after you created the leaf piles—rake off the top layer of leaves and beneath that will be a rich pile of compost gold ready to use.

- **Bagged Leaf Mold Compost** Rake a large amount of leaves together and shred them. Mix in a few shovels of rotted manure and water the pile well. Place this damp mixture in black plastic bags and punch a few holes in the bags for drainage. Place the bags along the south wall of a garage or home in full sun for the winter. Compost will be ready in the spring.

∧ Leaf mold does not look or smell like mold. Leaves decompose to create a rich compost filled with healthy microorganisms that are good for your garden beds.

CREATE CUSTOM COMPOST: GRASS CLIPPINGS

Dry it properly for rich benefits

GRASS CLIPPINGS MAKE GREAT COMPOST, but they create a lot of heat due to nitrogen decomposition. This means that putting fresh grass-clipping compost on your garden is much like using fresh manure: it burns plants instead of helping them. So the clippings must rot first (and off-site) in order to be most effective.

One of the best ways to hack grass clippings as compost is to benefit your lawn by using a mulching lawnmower. These machines have specially designed decks and blades that temporarily contain clippings as the machine mows, allowing the mower blades to slice them into much smaller pieces. These clippings then drop directly onto the yard as mulch, where they give back nitrogen and other nutrients to the soil. If you are a regular lawn mower and you keep your lawn cropped short, this technique is the easiest to manage. The benefits of using grass clippings on your lawn include lower levels of thatch and less pollution because compost reduces the need for fertilizers: approximately 50 percent of the lawn's annual fertilizer needs are taken care of by the site-generated mulch. There also is no need for bagging or lawn raking.

When using a mulching mower, be sure to mow when the lawn is dry so the grass does not stick to your blades. Remove no more than one-third of the grass height with each mowing, and if you must fertilize the lawn use organic fertilizers built specifically for grass.

A compost pile made exclusively from grass clippings can be challenging due to the intense heat created when the

< Placing a layer of grass clippings on top of a layer of composting browns in the compost bin will help build a hotter compost pile. *Photo credit: Ask Organic Online, www.askorganic.co.uk.*

clippings are at their peak in the breakdown cycle. Often, the decomposing grass will turn smelly and slimy because of the heat and moisture. By turning frequently, the grass will dry without smell.

Start with grass clippings that have not been exposed to chemicals such as non-organic fertilizers, herbicides, or pesticides. So the clippings don't become too matted or smelly, let them dry out for a couple of days before composting. Simply place the clippings in a pile and turn daily. Once dried, mix into your regular compost pile or create a mixture of 2 parts dry leaves and 1 part dry grass clippings. Place this grass/leaf mix in a well-aerated wire cage or a composter that lets a lot of air in and stir well. Keep slightly moist once mixed and turn weekly for the best results.

MAKE TURNING COMPOST EFFORTLESS
Easy tricks for introducing air

IT TAKES A LITTLE turning to make a compost pile produce faster. Efficient decomposition of the organic matter requires oxygen, and turning the pile creates air spaces that allow oxygen in. Introducing oxygen also decreases smelly anaerobic microbes that like to live in a dark, moist environment. As you turn the pile, you will notice that the volume of the materials will eventually reduce by about half. This is because the microbes eat and then excrete the remains of the compost material.

Aeration is as critical to a good compost pile as moisture, but compost can become very heavy and therefore challenging for a smaller person or a person with arthritis or another physical health condition to turn the compost effectively. Placing a shovel against the side of a small plastic composter and using the composter as a fulcrum, for example, can pop your composter apart or break the plastic edges of a composter. There are several hacks you can use to solve this problem:

- **Cranking compost turner** Cranking or screwing compost turners (see photo) enable you to drill down into the compost and with minimum force, lift the compost at the bottom of the composter through the middle up to the top. Remarkably easy to use, these compost cranks are helpful for people who have less upper body strength.
- **Auger** By using a cordless drill with a bulb auger attachment, you can easily hack your compost turn by screwing into the compost and pulling the material out much like a cranking or screwing compost turner.
- **Compost aerators** Compost aerators are mostly a series of harpoon-like tools that allow you to push forcefully into the compost, then pull up using a wide handle. At the bottom of the aerator are narrow metal brackets that lock open as you pull up and so bring up compost material too. These are excellent tools that truly help circulate materials with minimal physical effort.

- **Pitchforks** Garden forks or pitchforks are better for turning compost than shovels because you can stab into the compost with little resistance, lift it, and move it. Pitchforks work best if you have a large pile or a double composter where you can shift the compost from one bin to the other. To reduce the strain on your back, try gripping the fork closer to the tines.
- **Spinning composter** Finding a spinning composter is probably the easiest approach as you will need no tools whatsoever—just spin the composter regularly.

^ Spinning composters (right) and special screwing compost cranks (left) enable easier turning of a compost pile.

THE HACK-IT-UP HACK
Shredding makes compost break down faster

INTERESTED IN HACKING your compost so it decomposes more quickly? Make your compost ingredients smaller. Without a doubt, it is easier to turn compost ingredients that are cut up into smaller pieces, and the microbes and other creatures in the compost will consume smaller pieces more quickly. In order to create compost faster, follow these tips.

- **Mowing** Obviously, mowing over a pile of leaves, grass, garden debris, or weeds will chop the materials up into smaller bits. Build a pile about 1 foot high and as wide as needed, then turn your mower on and gently run over the material. If the material is too wet, the mower might bog down, so it is a smart practice to start with natural material that has had a little time to dry out. Pass over the pile several times in order to truly chop the bits up into small pieces.
- **Chippers and shredders** There are hundreds of wood chippers and material shredder devices in the garden marketplace. Large hunks of natural materials will not readily decompose, so shredding them completely before you place them in the compost pile is critical.
- **Chopping wet produce material** A great resource for your compost bin is to ask a local grocery store for all the produce it throws out on a daily basis. Most grocery stores throw out hundreds of pounds of produce per week. Because this material is wet, it does not do as well under a lawnmower, so you will have to lay it out on the ground and chop it up using a hand tool. Garden machetes or hori hori knives work great for this. Chop the pieces up as fine as you are able before throwing in the compost.
- **Urban living and worm composters** Living in an apartment or small home in an urban setting means that composting in large volumes is not possible. But you can gather your food and produce waste, slice it up in small hunks and/or

^ Chopping or shredding your compost ingredients will ensure a faster composting time.

grind pieces in a large blender or food scrap shredder, throw the material in a bag, then freeze it until you are ready to compost in order to prevent rotting smells in your household. Once you are ready, pull the frozen compost hunk out of the plastic and toss it in the composter.

14

BASIC DIY COMPOST BIN
The best bins are free and easy

HACKING A COMPOST bin is easy and can cost you absolutely nothing if you recycle and re-use old material. You can go fancy and more advanced, or you can go cheap and easy by recycling an old trash can. Either way, there is no excuse for living without a composter.

- **Old plastic bin composter** Have an old plastic storage tub that is 18 gallons or more with a tight-fitting lid? Perfect. Drill a dozen ½-inch holes in the bottom of the container for drainage and aeration. Make another dozen holes in the bin lid. Fill with your composting material. This is a great size composter for a balcony or patio as it is smaller and moveable.

- **Trash can composter** Use an old trash can with a tight-fitting lid. Drill 15 or 18 ½-inch to 1-inch holes in the sides of the plastic garbage can. Drill another 6 holes in the bottom of the can. Place the can on top of bricks to allow better drainage. Fill with your composting material. To mix the ingredients, roll the can around on the ground.

- **Any container with open sides** Make a wire composter with chicken wire formed into a circle. Or use milk crates stacked on top of one another, or build a container with old pallets, but make sure the pallets are chemical free for safer composting.

- **Fancy compost station** Making your own fancy compost station (see photo) is easy with 2×4s, screws, a few metal brackets, and wire. Using this photo as a general model, put together a three-part compost station. Make sure the station gets lots of air through the wire. In order to use this station most effectively, start the compost in the far right compost bin. When it fills three-quarters of the way full, turn the compost by using a pitchfork and moving the entire contents of the bin into the middle bin immediately to the left. Start filling the bin on the right again with more material. Repeat this process once the right bin gets full again, first moving the middle bin into the bin on the far left. When the compost reaches the far left bin, it should be ready for use.

> Building a composter with several compost bins makes it easier to turn the compost and aerate it when the compost is moved from one bin to the other. *Photo credit: Patricia Davis, The Gardeners Coach, www.gardenerscoach. wordpress.com.*

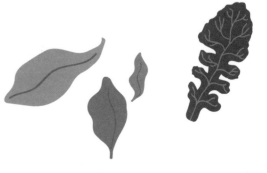

15

ROUND UP YOUR COMPOST COMPONENTS: THE BROWNS
Carbon-rich inputs give an energy boost

COMPOSTING IS MORE than just throwing all your food scraps in a pile. In order to have a successful composting experience, it is important to mix brown materials, green materials (see Hack 16: "Round Up Your Compost Components: The Greens"), air, and water together to create a healthy balance for the microbes to do their work and decompose the materials into healthy compost.

Brown materials for composting are typically the carbon sources that provides energy; they are also used for soaking up the extra moisture in a pile. Browns keep the heap aerated and helps prevent compaction of moister materials. Think of carbon-rich browns as being dry and nitrogen-rich greens as being wet, and it will help you better understand the formula.

Maintaining a carbon-to-nitrogen ratio close to 30 parts carbon to 1 part nitrogen will produce healthy compost quickly. Add too much nitrogen and you will have a hotter pile that might end up a stinky mess. Add too much carbon and decomposition slows down to a crawl, taking years to decompose. Finding that perfect combination is the challenge of all composters.

CARBON-RICH BROWNS

- Newspaper, black-and-white print preferred
- Brown paper bags from the grocery store
- Shredded cardboard and paper-based tissues, coffee filters, and towels
- Floor sweepings
- Straw
- Nut shells
- Aged and dried grass clippings
- Aged hay
- Pine needles
- Dead leaves; do not use dead leaves from diseased plants
- Wood chips and sticks
- Corn stalks
- 100-percent cotton cloth, cut into shreds
- Tea bags

> Modern-day newspapers are commonly printed with soy ink, which makes them a great addition to your compost's brown ingredients.

16

ROUND UP YOUR COMPOST COMPONENTS: THE GREENS

It's all about the nitrogen

^ Eggshells are high in calcium. Crushing the eggshells before you add them to the compost will help them break down more quickly in your composter.

GREEN MATERIALS FOR composting are typically bolder in color—like fruits, vegetables, and grass—and are also full of moisture. As discussed in the Compost Grass Clippings hack (see Hack 11), high-nitrogen ingredients like fresh grass clippings have the power to heat up the compost bin at such an extreme rate that if the aeration balance is not correct, your compost pile can become a slimy mess.

Variety also helps to keep the microorganisms happy in your compost pile. A variety of different carbon-rich browns and nitrogen-rich greens are important to support your compost pile.

There are many other materials that might be rich in nitrogen or carbon, but you should not put them in your compost pile because the results might harm you. Do not include sludge or biosolids, fish bones and scraps, meat, cat litter, pet or human wastes, nut butters, glossy or colored paper, charcoal, fatty waste and greasy foods, or dairy products.

CHOOSE FROM THESE NITROGEN-RICH GREENS

- New grass clippings
- Plant prunings; do not add prunings from diseased plants
- Hair
- Spent flowers and pulled weeds
- Coffee grounds
- Tea grounds
- Bone meal
- Kitchen scraps; avoid excessive citrus items and material that will root, such as potato skins and onions, unless ground completely
- Crushed eggshells
- Blood meal
- Barnyard animal manure (cow, horse, chicken, goat, sheep, and rabbit; do not use dog, cat, or human manure/feces as they may contain pathogens or diseases that could be harmful)
- Worm castings
- Feathers
- Alfalfa meal
- Wet hay
- Young hedge trimmings
- Freshwater algae and untreated aquarium water
- Seaweed; rinse the seaweed with water before adding to the pile in order to remove excess salt

MAINTENANCE
hacks

HACKS IN THIS CHAPTER

DISCOVER THE POWER OF EPSOM SALT
A fast-acting affordable fertilizer

EPSOM SALT, or magnesium sulfate, is named for the town where it was discovered: Epsom, England. This product has been used to treat ailments and fertilize plants for more than a hundred years. Applying this mineral to your garden is an inexpensive fertilizer hack that has a big impact on your plants.

Before you consider applying Epsom salt to your garden, it is important to have your soil tested to determine whether it is actually magnesium deficient. Adding too much Epsom salt to your garden is adding excessive magnesium to your beds. Therefore, test the soil first and if you do have a deficiency, Epsom salt can help correct the problem, but it won't be adequate for very large soil deficiencies. Magnesium deficiency in plants is usually seen as leaf yellowing, leaf curling, and stunted growth. An added magnesium component allows plants to better absorb nutrients such as phosphorus and nitrogen. Some plants, such as tomatoes and peppers, perform better with a consistent magnesium amendment. Here are specific ways to use Epsom salt.

∧ Epsom salt has many uses in the garden; you can find it in grocery, drug, and hardware stores.

- **Soil** At the beginning of garden season, broadcast 1 cup of Epsom salt per 100 square feet of garden bed.
- **General foliar spray** Epsom salt works well when diluted with water and applied as a foliar spray that is taken up quickly by the plant. Mix 2 tablespoons per gallon of rainwater and apply one time per month. Drench the base of the plants with any leftover solution at the soil level.
- **Vegetable plants** For vegetable garden plants, apply 1 tablespoon of Epsom salt granules at the base of each plant. Follow that with a foliar spray of 1 tablespoon per gallon of water once per month.
- **Roses** In a bucket, soak rose roots in a solution of ½ cup of Epsom salt mixed with 1 gallon of water. Top-dress roses with 1 tablespoon of Epsom salt around the root area of the plant.

BREW A BATCH OF MANURE TEA
Its uses are many, its price is not steep

THE EFFECTIVENESS OF manure tea is one of the most hotly debated garden discussions. While many scientists contend that manure tea is not an effective soil amendment, the vast hordes of gardeners who have applied a dose to their plants disagree vehemently because they have seen the positive results. Manure tea is filled with aerobic bacteria and has been used for centuries as a valuable and economical fertilizer. Typically, it is made from a hot, nitrogen-rich manure. This creates a positive soil amendment for heavy garden feeders that require additional nutrition throughout the season; among these are asparagus, tomatoes, and peppers.

Remember: *Do not drink this tea.* It's only to be used as a soil conditioner for your plants. Water your plants with the tea, and be sure sprinkle it on the leaves as it is also absorbed through the leaf system as well as through the soil.

< Fill a watering can or bucket with rainwater, toss in a manure tea bag, let steep, and then feed your plants with manure tea for a healthy garden.

- **Homemade manure tea** The best manures to use for homemade tea include cow, horse, goat, and rabbit manures. Put a shovel-full of rotted, composted manure in a large burlap or cotton sack and close the sack with twine tied tightly at the top of the sack. Fill a 5-gallon bucket with rainwater. Put the manure sack in the water. Stir occasionally. Steep in the water for three to five days until the tea is a deep brown color. Dilute your homemade manure tea by half so you do not burn your plants. Use one to two times per week throughout the growing season when watering.

- **Pre-made manure tea bags** Brands such as the Authentic Haven Brand tea bag provide a no-fuss and no-mess way of making manure tea. Simply fill a watering can or 5-gallon bucket with rainwater, toss in a tea bag, and let steep for one to three days until the tea is a deep brown color. There is no need to dilute this tea; pour directly into a watering can and water your thirsty plants.

GROUNDS FOR GROWTH
Coffee grounds do not add acid but do add humic properties

COMMON COFFEE GROUNDS have many beneficial effects in the garden. According to Dr. Linda Chalker-Scott, Associate Professor at Washington State University:

> Humic substances, which are important chemical and structural soil components, are produced through coffee ground degradation. Carbon-to-nitrogen ratios change as well, generally starting out a bit higher than ideal (e.g. 25–26) and decreasing to 21, 13, 11, or even 9.4 in a year's time. Less straightforward are the changes in pH that occur during decomposition. A commonly held assumption states that coffee grounds are acidic, but this does not hold true experimentally. While two studies on coffee ground composting reported mildly acidic pH levels of 4.6 and 5.26, others have measured neutral (7.7) to somewhat alkaline (8.4) pH levels. One researcher found that the pH level of soil treated with coffee compost rose after 14 to 21 days of incubation, gradually decreasing thereafter. Obviously the pH of decomposing coffee grounds is not stable and one shouldn't assume that it will reliably, if ever, be acidic.

Coffee grounds appear to suppress some common fungal rots and wilts, and at the same time they have proven to be an effective replacement for peat moss (an endangered resource). But the best use for this ubiquitous kitchen waste is simply to add it to your garden compost. If you are not a regular imbiber of coffee drinks made at home, go to your local coffee shop and ask them to save their coffee grounds for you—they are usually happy to get the coffee grounds out of their waste stream and also to keep them out of the landfill. Add coffee grounds (you can even include unbleached paper filters) to your compost pile liberally, but the volume of grounds should not exceed 10 to 20 percent of the total volume of your compost pile or bin.

∧ Coffee grounds are an excellent compost ingredient. Add to your compost at a 10 to 20 percent ratio to the total volume of the pile.

WASH YOUR MOTHS OUT WITH SOAP?
Mix a batch of soap-based insecticide

SUPPLIES NEEDED
- Clean spray bottle
- Pure soap; all-natural or castile works well, do not use oil-based dish soap
- Water

HOW TO
1. Mix 1 tablespoon of soap in 1 quart of water in spray bottle.
2. Shake well.
3. Spray.

WITHOUT A DOUBT, the best way to prevent insect damage to your plants is to discourage them from coming to your garden. This can be accomplished with a few simple steps: Keep plant foliage as dry as possible. Clean up weedy undergrowth, and pull weak plants that might be diseased (insects often attack the weak plants first and live in the messy undergrowth and garden debris). Rotate vegetable and herb crops annually, and encourage beneficial insects.

When prevention does not work, however, look for organic solutions, such as handpicking Japanese beetles or spraying off aphids with a powerful hose burst; these are effective treatments with no negative side effects. Another option is homemade insecticidal soap. Free of chemicals (and practically free to make), soapy water is my favorite treatment for soft-bodied insects such as whiteflies, aphids, mealybugs, mites, and thrips. Fatty acid from the soap melts the insects' cell membranes, so spraying directly on the bug is critical for this all-natural solution to work. The soapy film left behind on the plant leaves also discourages other insects from taking a bite.

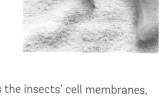

˅ Pure castile soap mixed with water makes a wonderful homemade insecticidal soap that will help rid your garden of insects.

WHAT'S SO BAD ABOUT INSECTICIDE?

Over 5 billion pounds of pesticides are used in agriculture worldwide; over $31.8 billion was spent in 2001 alone to protect against insects. While some pesticides are useful, many kill both the good bugs and the bad bugs in the garden. Choosing to garden without heavy pesticides means you are taking a step toward better environmental practices by allowing the beneficial insects, which are necessary for a healthier garden, to survive and do their job. There are many reasons to go without pesticides in your garden. For example, insects feed other animals in the food chain, such as birds, so can be useful to a gardener who enjoys home bird watching.

EZ EARWIG TRAP HACKS
Two simple tricks to combat these garden pests

EARWIGS ARE SCARY-LOOKING insects. In the Middle Ages, they were rumored to use their pinchers to crawl into the ears of sleeping people, burrow into their brains, and lay eggs. This is, of course, a myth. Earwigs are not known to bite or attack humans. But they can do plenty of damage to your garden.

Earwigs are outdoor nocturnal insects that feed on rotted or decaying plant material that is usually found in damp areas beneath rotted wood, dead leaves, and mulch.

They also attack tender-leaved plants, such as hostas and new vegetables, using their abdominal forceps pincers to incise the leaf so they can feed on the cut material. Earwigs can do serious damage to an entire crop, so must be controlled immediately when discovered.

The first signs of earwig damage are usually cut holes in the leaves that look a lot like slug damage. To determine whether you have earwigs or slugs, use a garden hose

< Earwigs might be the pest that is attacking your tender plants in the garden; they are notorious for leaving holes in the leaves and can damage entire crops overnight.

to wet down an area in your garden that is showing leaf damage. Wait until late night, then go out to the garden location with the lights off, raise your leaves up, and flash a light on the plant. If you see earwigs scurrying away, you will know they are the root of the damage, not the relatively slow-footed slug. If instead of a pack of earwigs you see slimy slug or snail trials, focus your abatement plans on these creatures (see Hack 72: "Keep Slugs out of Planting Containers").

Once you've determined that you have earwigs in your garden, here are a couple of easy hacks you can deploy to dispense with them:

- **Baited traps** Put a mixture of 3 parts water, 1 part soy sauce, and 1 teaspoon molasses in a small container—like an old yogurt or butter container—and shake it up. In the evening, dig a hole in the area where the earwigs are attacking your plants and sink the small container in the soil so the top is level with the ground. Gently pour vegetable oil over the top of the liquid so it forms a very thin layer. Come back the next morning and discover hundreds of earwigs in the container. Discard the container and the pests.
- **Rolled-up newspaper trap** Lay a sheet of newspaper flat and roll it up length-wise. Take it to the problematic area in the garden in the late evening. Place it on the ground, then soak the area well with a water hose. Go out in the very early morning and collect the newspaper. Either shake the earwigs out in a soapy bucket, or throw the newspaper away in a plastic bag tied tightly so no bugs can escape.

Keep in mind that earwigs are attracted to moist areas, so cleaning up wet or damp areas in the garden can help keep them away from your plants. Female earwigs can lay 20 to 60 eggs per season, so one session of trapping will not work. It is essential to lay traps repeatedly every night for a week, then repeat the process again in a few weeks' time in order to seriously reduce the earwig population.

MAKE A CASTINGS CALL
Homegrown or store bought, worm castings work

WORM CASTINGS ARE actually worm manure or worm excreta. Known to increase microbial activity around a plant root zone, worm castings are filled with beneficial micronutrients and trace minerals. Worm castings do not have an odor, hold two to three times their weight in water, will not burn your plants, are safe for pets and children, and are water soluble and immediately available to plant life. Worm castings are so amazingly powerful, that you will need five times as much potting soil to do the same job as worm castings.

One surprising aspect of worm castings is that they have the ability to fix heavy metals in organic waste, which means when used in quantity, worm castings will prevent a plant's absorption of heavy metal chemicals. Use them liberally mixed in with your mulch, and follow the instructions below for compost and soil amendments.

∧ Worm castings should be mixed in with your soil at planting time or made into a manure tea for an added dose of organic nutrition throughout the garden season.

- **Compost** In order to mix the correct ratio of worm castings in a compost bin, Mark Highland, founder and president of Organic Mechanics Soil, recommends an occasional compost layer of about 1 pound of worm castings. He says it is best to "sprinkle it on top of a brown layer much like you were sprinkling powdered sugar on top of a donut."
- **Ground planting** Mix ¼ cup into each planting hole for all plants in order to assist them with root establishment. Also use the castings as a topdressing for outdoor plants.

- **Container planting** Mix ¼ cup of worm castings into every gallon of organic soil. Because worm castings have the remarkable ability to absorb and hold moisture, this addition can strongly improve a drought-tolerant container planting. Additional top-dressing throughout the season is beneficial for container plantings.
- **Worm casting tea** In order to make worm casting tea, mix 1 gallon of water with 1 pound of worm castings. Shake or stir. Use immediately if you like, or let sit for 24 hours for a richer tea.

BEYOND BEER

Several solutions to solving a slug problem

> One reliable way slugs can be readily controlled is by handpicking the creatures out of your garden.

SLUGS ARE BOTHERSOME and horrid garden pests found all around the world. Technically, a slug is a mollusk that lacks a shell and secretes a slimy covering of mucus for protection. While some slugs are predatory and eat other slugs, worms, or snails, most species prefer feeding on a wide variety of organic materials, particularly prized plants in your garden. Once your garden is infested with slugs, it can be hard to get rid of them because a slug lays between 20 to 100 eggs several times a year and is hermaphroditic, meaning it has both male and female reproductive organs. One individual slug can produce more than 90,000 grandchildren.

In a recent "How to Control Slugs Organically" poll by *Mother Earth News*, 87 percent of respondents said handpicking was the best way to control slugs. Beer bait, iron phosphate bait, and diatomaceous earth followed as highly successful organic control. However, an eggshell barrier, which is created by sprinkling crushed eggshells around plants to cut the skin of a slug, had a 33 percent failure rate. Predatory control also works, specifically with chickens and ducks.

Diatomaceous earth, or DE, is made from diatoms (fossilized algae), which is finely ground into dust. In order to prevent slugs, apply a 1- to 1½-inch wide band of DE around plants after a heavy rain. When either slugs or snails crawl over the dust, it sticks to them and causes their bodies to dry out. Be sure to use goggles, gloves, and a dust mask during application.

Prevention is the best control for slugs, which means eliminating dark, moist hiding areas around the garden and increasing air circulation. Trimming and limbing-up trees in order to get stronger sunlight exposure can help. Clean up rotting undergrowth and excessive mulch from the garden.

BECOME A JAPANESE BEETLE COLLECTOR
A handpicked hack for controlling garden bugs

JAPANESE BEETLES ARE invasive pests that were originally introduced to the United States in 1908 and have since become a crop-devastating scourge. They love roses, raspberries, grapes, beans, hollyhocks, and hundreds of other garden plants. Identifiable by their metallic copper-and-green shells, the signs of their presence will be obvious: total defoliation or skeletonized leaves on all variety of plants in your garden.

They are only around for about four weeks of the summer, but when they are in your garden you must keep a constant vigil. Japanese beetles sometimes feed in large groups, starting at the top of plants, so finding them will be easy—and they do not bite humans so are easy to snatch off the plants. Handpicking the creatures and throwing them in soapy water is the best way to organically control them. Insecticidal soap spray will kill the beetles, but you must spray the beetles directly, so it is just as easy to locate them and knock them into a vat of soapy water rather than spray.

If you have large and repeated infestations, it would be best to check your soil in late summer to discover the grub population count. Certain grubs turn into Japanese beetles. It is easy to get a count by lifting a square-foot section of turf and checking to see if you discover more than 12 grubs or so in the area. If so, you can try treating your lawn with some form of organic grub control such as milky spore and nematodes. Using Japanese beetle traps within 500 to 600 yards of susceptible plants will simply attract more beetles in to your garden. Therefore it is not recommended unless the trap is a significant distance from your plants or you work together with neighbors to do community-wide trapping. Beetles collected in traps should be frozen and can then be fed to animals such as chickens or pond fish.

∧ Japanese beetles are easily identifiable by their metallic copper and green hard shells.

STAY AWAY FROM TOXIC TOOLS
Yes, there is such a thing as a greener garden hose

TRADITIONAL GARDEN HOSES have recently come under fire because high levels of hazardous chemicals were discovered in tests conducted by the internationally recognized Ecology Center in Ann Arbor, Michigan. If the water was left sitting in certain hoses in the sun for a few days, heavy amounts of phthalates and BPA were found. Additionally, PVC and hazardous metals were found in hoses including lead, tin stabilizers, and antimony.

By using traditional chemical-filled hoses, the vegetables and herbs you water over the season will be contaminated with these toxic chemicals. There are several steps you can take to have an organic garden hose experience:

- **Purchase a PVC-free hose** that is specifically labeled as "drinking water safe" or "lead free."
- **Avoid hoses that post warnings** on the packaging such as, "This product contains a chemical known to the State of California to cause cancer and birth defects and other reproductive harm."
- As an added safety concern, **never drink water from a hose** even if it says it is drinking water safe, and do not let your pets drink this water.

∧ Use drinking water-safe hoses in your garden and your garden plants will be exposed to lower doses of chemicals.

- **Let the water run** through your hose for a few seconds before using on food plants growing in your garden because water that has been sitting in the hose has the highest level of chemical leaching.

PACK YOUR PLANTS IN TIGHTLY
Intensive planting boosts yield and saves water

INTENSIVE PLANTING TECHNIQUES are practiced with several goals in mind: They minimize soil compaction, allow you to plant in challenging or difficult locations, solve drainage issues, eliminate the need for tilling, increase vegetable and herb production, and conserve water. With many parts of the world suffering from drought, it is critical to find a way to use less water and still grow more produce in less space. Intensive planting techniques can accomplish all these things and more.

Preparing your soil for a no-till garden situation is vitally important to an intensive-planted garden (see Hack 1: "Retire Your Tiller") because the basis for a garden like this is a deeply fertile and well-drained soil. Using organic mulches, rotted manure, and rich compost as soil amendments is the foundation to a fabulous intensively planted garden.

There are several long-standing techniques for intensive planting that have proven to be very successful, including square-foot gardening and bio-intensive gardening. The

no-till, richly fertile technique of bio-intensive gardening, combined with simply planting more plants, creates a special environment for your vegetable or herb plants that helps hold water at the roots for a longer period of time. This, in turn, creates a setting in which the plants help support one another. In the photo on this page you see three raised beds packed full of plants—collard greens, mustard greens, and celery—all growing quite successfully with minimal water.

Careful advance planning is the key to success with this water-saving technique. Plant herbs and vegetables in strips 1 to 3 feet wide using elevated or raised beds that are about 12 inches above ground level. Leave the side of the beds open or use a raised bed system. Packing the plants closer together without overplanting is important. Mulching and thinning the plants as necessary to prevent disease and pests is also critical because tightly planted gardens also have reduced air circulation. Succession planting will help extend your gardening season.

< Here are three raised beds filled with collard greens, mustard greens, and celery utilizing the intensive-planting technique. Plants share space with a minimum use of water.

MAKE AND USE A "POOR MAN'S OLLA"
A modern hack of a traditional irrigation tool

FOR MORE THAN 4,000 years, many cultures in China and Northern Africa have been utilizing ollas (pronounced *OY-yahs*) as watering tools. This technique, which is still practiced today, involves burying an unglazed clay or terra-cotta pot in the ground with the neck of the pot exposed, but the bottom of the pot resting near the plant roots. The result is a type of primitive sub-surface irrigation that is very easy to adapt to modern gardens.

Particularly effective in drylands and drought-ridden regions, ollas allow water to gently seep in the direction where underground suction forms near root systems.

Ollas help eliminate runoff and evaporation, which is predominant with modern irrigation systems. Water savings can be as much as 50 to 70 percent, which is particularly advantageous for vegetable and herb gardening. In addition, less fertilizer is needed and less labor is required because you do not have to water as frequently.

If you do not have access to a genuine clay olla, it is easy to make a "Poor Man's Olla" with an old milk carton. Small cartons can be used in container gardens and raised beds, while gallon-sized milk jugs can be used in your traditional garden beds.

HOW TO MAKE A "POOR MAN'S OLLA"
1. Rinse an empty plastic milk jug and punch 6 to 8 very small holes from the top to the bottom on all four sides of the jug.
2. Dig a hole within 4 to 5 inches of a plant, or in the middle of several plants that are all within 4 to 5 inches away from the hole.
3. Bury the milk jug up to the top of its handle, or preferably its neck, leaving the mouth of the container available to be filled with water.
4. Fill the jug with water. Your poor man's olla should be half full at all times to work most effectively and keep the plastic from collapsing.

< Bury a milk jug up to the top of its handle or its neck, leaving the lid on. Open the lid and fill with water; keep it at least half full at all times.

SELF-WATERING CONTAINERS
Two pots and a plastic cup are all you need

WATERING PLANTS IN containers can be a time-consuming chore, particularly in the heat and wind of summer. Making your own self-watering containers is a great way to hack a watering system. Typically, commercially available self-watering garden containers have an area to hold the plants and soil, then a bottom pot or reservoir that holds excess water. Some form of wick will link the inner and outer pot so that water is drawn up to the plant roots as the moisture level in the soil decreases.

Hacking your own self-watering container is easily done. Find two planting containers the same size; place a yogurt or butter tub in between the two containers to create a water reservoir; drill extra holes in the "inner" planting container base; and feed a piece of cotton rope through one of the holes into the bottom water reservoir. Fill the reservoir with a hose or watering can by lifting the container or by cutting a feed hole to help supply water.

This technique works great on a balcony, fire escape, or patio. Filling your reservoir with rainwater when possible is a wise choice as there are fewer chemicals in rainwater compared to city water or softened water. Never use softened water in your container gardens because the dissolved salts are toxic to your plants. Most self-watering containers are food safe, but do your research and make sure this is true before planting in a self-watering unit.

> Self-watering containers are a time-saving garden hack because you spend less time watering and more time growing.

INSTALL A DRIP LINE KIT FOR
CONTAINER OR RAISED-BED GARDENS
An easy DIY project that saves countless hours of hand-watering

WATERING WITH HOSES leads to a fair amount of water loss due to evaporation. By running drip lines to your container gardens, you save an immense amount of water and will be more successful with your container plantings with far less effort. No need to hire a professional landscaping team to install your system: you can hack this project yourself easy-peasy and take the worry out of watering, especially if you add a timer.

Industrial container drip systems have long been used in greenhouses; it's a simple system that works. Most drip systems have a filter to keep particles from clogging the tubes—cleaning this filter is the only consistent maintenance chore related to drip systems for your container gardens.

HOW TO INSTALL A DRIP LINE KIT

1. Calculate the layout of your container plants and how many you want to have irrigated.
2. Purchase a prepackaged drip system package built for container gardens and that will accommodate your plan. Get a kit that includes a timer, filter, pressure regulator, and anti-siphon device; extra tubing is a bonus as being able to cut custom lengths is important.
3. Run a drinking water-safe hose from your outdoor water source to the general area where the container gardens will be placed.
4. Water pressure declines if there are too many containers attached to the circuit. Try to build a tight circuit of less than 50 feet with ¼-inch tubing and a maximum of 12 to 15 gallons per hour of emitter output. Larger tubing enables you to expand your footage and increase emitter output.
5. Once the system is set up, set the timer, check for leaks, and make sure there is enough water being delivered to the plants.
6. Check every few months for clogs and flush the line for up to a minute.
7. Turn the system off and disassemble it during winter months if the weather in your region consistently gets below 35°F.

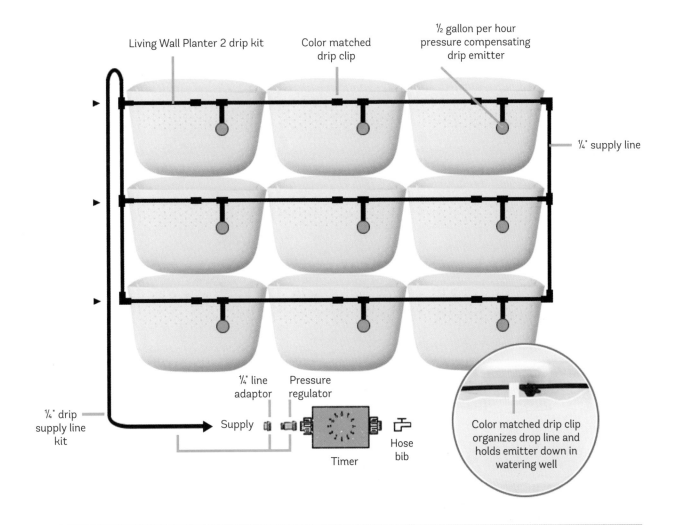

Living Wall Planter 2 drip kit

Color matched drip clip

½ gallon per hour pressure compensating drip emitter

¼" supply line

¼" line adaptor

Pressure regulator

¼" drip supply line kit

Supply

Timer

Hose bib

Color matched drip clip organizes drop line and holds emitter down in watering well

∧ Drip lines for garden containers, living walls, and raised beds are easy to assemble if you lay out your units and follow package directions for the drip system product. *Illustration credit: This illustrative drip line design is for the Living Wall Planter 2 container system from www.woollypocket.com.*

HARVEST THE RAIN

Rain barrel water isn't just free, it's better for your plants

IN ORDER TO take advantage of free rainwater, install a rain barrel system with one or more rain barrels (see photo), or create your own rain barrel for a next-to-nothing cost by converting a trash can.

Harvesting rain is very important to you and your community. An average US household with an average-sized lot uses up to 3,000 gallons of water weekly for landscape irrigation. Collecting rainwater for use in your garden means you don't have to purchase that water. Also, it costs millions of dollars of taxpayer money to maintain and repair public storm water and sewer systems. By collecting your own water and withholding it from storm water systems, you save yourself and the community money. Approximately 1 inch of rainfall on a 2,000-square-foot roof creates 1,250 gallons of water that can be reused by your household. Over time, it is possible to collect thousands of useable gallons of water for free from your rooftop.

Plants watered with rainwater are not exposed to chlorine and other chemicals that most municipalities add to tap water. While water from a rainwater cistern is considered non-potable because it has not been chemically treated, it is magnificent to use for our plants, as they will not have to absorb additional chemicals (such as chlorine and fluoride).

∧ Dual rain barrel systems allow you to collect more rain water for your garden. Hack your own rain barrel by using a trash can for a no- to low-cost solution.

HOW TO MAKE A TRASH CAN RAIN BARREL

1. Drill one hole the size of the spigot you have purchased in the bottom front of a 32-gallon or larger garbage can and another hole the size of your overflow garden hose at the top rear of the garbage can.
2. Attach a spigot piece to the front lower hole with sealant and washers.
3. Attach a short overflow garden hose on the top rear hole, also using sealant and washers.
4. Cut a hole in the lid for water entry from the rain gutter drain; cover with a piece of screen.
5. Place your empty garbage can below the rain gutter drain and position on cement blocks so that the rain barrel sits up higher than ground level. By raising the gravity-fed system up higher, it will enable the water to flow more briskly to the garden if you attach a hose to the spigot.

31

CHANGE WINE BOTTLES INTO WATER BOTTLES

A quick hack to provide slow-release water

ALL GARDENERS HAVE a few plants, either planted in the garden or in a garden container, that require a little extra water attention. What is a gardener to do when faced with business travel and an active lifestyle and no time to water? Hack garden watering by using a wine bottle watering system: it is also a fantastic way to conserve water while helping that difficult plant along.

Wine bottle watering works with a trickle-down principle to provide a consistent and steady supply of water to the plant's root system. There are several watering spike systems that allow you to connect a water, soda, or wine bottle to a pointy spike that is then inserted into the soil. Included in this genre are terracotta stakes (see photo), plastic screw-on tops, or bottle lid adapters. Any of these are easy to use unless the garden container is too small; the weight of a bottle filled with water can tip the container. Therefore, this hack is best used in larger containers or directly in the ground.

To use a bottle without a spike adapter, simply dig a small hole about the size of the neck of the wine bottle next to the plant that needs a little extra love and tender care. Do not disturb the plant's roots, but place the hole as close to the root system as you can get. Water the area well before you place the bottle in the soil. Fill the bottle with water, then quickly turn it upside down, and insert the neck into the hole and backfill around the bottle with soil so it is well supported.

∧ Creating a bottle watering system is easy and can be quite decorative if you use a bottle with bold, attractive colors.

Watering frequency with this technique depends on the rate of water trickle, how large the bottle is, and what the weather conditions are at the moment. Test it out the first week or two by putting your fingers on the ground between the plant and bottle. If it is cool and slightly moist, the bottle is doing its job. If it is dry, the bottle needs to be refilled with water and replaced in the hole.

THREE SHADES OF GREYWATER

Reuse cooking water in the garden

THROWING OUT YOUR cooking water without recycling it is wasting an opportunity in three ways: You lose a nutritional supplement for plants, valuable moisture, and a weed killer. Finding creative ways to reuse water means you are doing your part for the betterment of the environment. Try the easy hacks below and make a difference.

∧ Once vegetables, hard-boiled eggs, and other foods have been cooked, let the water cool and use it as a supplement to your garden. Boiling water is excellent for kiling weeds.

- **Plant nutrition and fertilizer** Depending on what you are cooking, nutritious aspects leach into the cooking water. If, for instance, you make hard-boiled eggs, there will be an excess of calcium in the water. Let the egg water cool, then water your calcium-loving plants such as tomatoes, peppers, and tomatillos, with the water. Boiling greens such as spinach or chard will produce iron-enhanced water. Potatoes and pasta starch is also good for your garden, but heavy salts are not, so do not use salted water.
- **Water savings** In an area of the world where drought is a concern, using your cooled cooking water as an additional source of water is genius. Simply remove whatever you were cooking, let the water cool to room temperature, and then carry it to the garden and distribute it. This same idea can work with your dishwater if you use an all-natural, non-oil-based soap.
- **Kill weeds** Boiling water is a great weed killer. Have a driveway or sidewalk filled with weeds? No problem. Remove whatever you were cooking in the pan, then heat the water up again to boiling. Using hot pads, carry the boiling water to your weedy sidewalk and slowly pour the water over the crowns of the weeds.

33

ORGANIC WASP CONTROL

If you can't ignore them, trap them

OUTDOOR LIFE ON patios and in gardens means you sometimes run into a wasp situation. Wasps are very good for the environment because they function as pollinators. As a policy, try not to harm wasps. However, for the safety of your pets and family, if you have to control wasps, there are way to do it without chemicals. Eliminating the things that wasps are attracted to is a great way to prevent stings. This includes rotting garbage, fruit from fruit trees, sweet foods and drinks, compost piles, heavy perfumes, and pet food.

When you see a wasp, do not run or swat. If there are only one or two wasps, stay calm and very still. Wait for the wasps to fly off. If there is a swarm of wasps and they have stung already, calmly cover your face with your hands and slowly back away from the swarming wasps. Do not run, even if you feel panicked. Seek treatment immediately.

When a wasp lands on you, do not run or swat. Gently wipe the wasp off of you with paper or cardboard—not your hand. Slowly walk away without panicking.

While it's best not to kill wasps, it is sometimes necessary. In those instances, it is much safer to use a trap rather than insecticide. While the insecticide is deadly to the wasps, it is also harmful to humans when inhaled and not good at all for the environment.

∧ Wasp nests can be found in the smallest of places. While wasps are great pollinators in the garden, sometimes controls must be taken to manage them.

HOW TO BUILD AN ALL-NATURAL WASP TRAP

1. Get an empty 2-liter plastic bottle.
2. Cut the top third off of the bottle and turn it upside down.
3. Insert the upside-down portion into the bottle.
4. Securely tape the bottle pieces together.
5. Fill with fruit juice to attract wasps.
6. Set the bottle near the nest and away from high-traffic areas in your garden. (Hanging it after dark means the wasps will be less active and not as likely to sting.)
7. Wasps enter the upside-down cone, but cannot find a way out.

HOW TO ORGANICALLY SPRAY DOWN A WASP NEST

1. Wait until evening when all the wasps return to the nest.
2. Put ¼ cup pure castile soap in a hose-end sprayer.
3. Run the water until you see suds.
4. Spray the nest with a powerful spray. Stop to see if they are still flying. If so, spray again.
5. Repeat the process the next evening if you are still concerned that the insects might still be alive.

POLLINATOR hacks

HACKS IN THIS CHAPTER

34

PLANT WITH AN EYE TOWARD POLLINATORS
The bees, birds, and butterflies (and your fruiting plants) will thank you

EVERY GARDENER SHOULD heed this advice: plant flowering native plants such as butterfly weed, Joe-pye weed, and gayfeather to support local indigenous pollinators. It is easier than ever before to garden with local native plants. Lists of local plant varieties can be found at any local extension office or local independent garden center.

Many gardens in the United States feature plants that might not support pollinators as readily as others. Changing the entire garden over to organic, native-pollinating plants may be an unreasonable transition. Gradually intermixing native annuals and perennials can help attract and feed pollinating insects. Be sure to plant pollen- and nectar-rich plants with successive flowering seasons so that the plants can help provide for pollinators all season.

Annual plants bring in pollinators, but they do not return year after year and so can't help support the pollinators for the long term. Great annuals that support butterflies, bees, and hummingbirds include zinnia, flowering tobacco, lantana, and verbena. Non-native perennial plants that are particularly attractive to bees include bee balm, catmint, anise hyssop, lavender, oregano, and salvia.

Let a few of your container and in-ground plants bolt; herbs, vegetables, and foliage annuals that are allowed to flower, such as coleus, are also wonderful nectar sources for pollinators. You can also let basil, mint, marjoram, oregano, and other plants bolt early on in the season, and you will benefit the pollinator community.

WHY DOES POLLINATOR SUPPORT MAKE A DIFFERENCE?

Pollinator insects, birds, and animals are incredibly important to our ecosystem. A recent scientific study conducted by the University of Sussex's Laboratory of Apiculture and Social Insects proved that including organically grown native and non-native pollinator-friendly flowers in your garden can attract and help support bees and other insects. This is important for gardeners everywhere because it is possible to add a small number of pollinating plants to your garden and make a positive impact on your local pollinator population.

∧ Zinnias attract butterflies, hummingbirds, and bees. They are an excellent addition to the organic herb or vegetable garden to help bring more pollinators into the garden.

SEND A SHOUT-OUT TO HUMMINGBIRDS
Feeders and plant selection will bring these treasures into your yard

TO ATTRACT AND keep hummingbirds in your garden, it is important to grow plants they love. Tubular flowers that enable a hummingbird to sup are good, and native plants are always the first choice. Research native plants that are suitable for your region at your local nursery. Consider planting other common hummingbird favorites such as gayfeather, cardinal flower, flowering tobacco, salvia, bee balm, catmint, columbine, coral bells, pincushion flowers, verbena, weigela, and zinnia. Maintaining a hummingbird feeder also attracts the birds. Hang the feeder well away from predator access and near a water source.

Hummingbirds like exceptionally clean feeders. Change the nectar about every two weeks; wash them thoroughly with soap and water. Many experts suggest changing the nectar even more frequently—every three days or so. Watch your feeders carefully and keep them as clean as possible. While some people insist on boiling the nectar before placing it out, that is not absolutely necessary. Try shaking the water and sugar together until all the sugar melts. Put the feeders out in the garden very early—as soon as the snow melts—in order to have them available for early scout birds. If you get ants or bees invading the feeders, simply add a bit of petroleum jelly around the opening of each feeding hole or move your feeder to a different location.

HOW TO MAKE HUMMINGBIRD NECTAR FORMULA
1. Mix 1 part organic sugar to 4 parts water.
2. Shake well or boil and let cool.
3. Pour into a clean hummingbird feeder.
4. Replace biweekly or whenever the feeder runs empty.

∧ Hummingbirds love the color red, but there is no need to use artificial dyes to color their nectar: simply use a red bottle or feeding tube with a red flower on it as an attraction accent.

WHAT'S SO GREAT ABOUT HUMMINGBIRDS?
Small, colorful, and iridescent, hummingbirds are found all over the world. They weigh less than an ounce, and when they beat their wings at about 80 times per second while in flight, they make a delightful humming noise. Hummingbirds have a long, thin bill that they use to reach nectar from tubular flowers. Without a doubt, these little birds have become a gardener's favorite friend because of their territorial antics and delightful personalities.

36

GROW A BEE FLOWER:
HOW ABOUT A HARDY GERANIUM?

Make a statement with the plants you choose

∧ Bees love perennial geraniums of all varieties and spend hours in the garden tending to the delicate flowers.

HARDY PERENNIAL GERANIUMS are flush with flowers and pollinators all through the early spring season. They rebloom consistently and love shade and woodland sites, which makes them perfect for supporting bees of all types. Hardy perennial geranium is not the tender *Pelargonium geranium* we remember from our grandmothers' gardens. There are many types of hardy geraniums: some are low-growing and make perfect groundcovers for tight spaces; larger varieties can easily stretch to 4 feet tall and wide. While most geraniums prefer sun to part sun, a number of them will easily perform in the shade. Choose the planting site based upon the variety of geranium you have chosen and its sun exposure preferences.

Although geraniums do not like standing in water, they do like a consistent medium moisture and a humus-rich soil with lots of natural items mixed in: Rotted manure, compost, and worm castings make perfect soil amendments. This does not make them a likely candidate for hot or arid areas in the garden. Plant them directly into rich soil or containers in spring after the last frost, or plant them from seed in the fall or in the spring if the geranium seed has been cold treated.

Hardy geraniums make a surprising sound when seeds explode from seed pods in latent flower heads. Plants throw seeds quite a distance after the flowering has ended in early summer.

The geranium can be divided by digging up the rhizomes and cutting them between arising stems. A new cluster of basal leaves and flowering stems will crop up from the thick, branched horizontal rhizomes. Water them regularly upon initial transplanting. Once they are established, geraniums will survive dry conditions as long as the soil is rich.

Prune back flower stems after the first bloom to help tidy the plant and encourage it to bloom again. Prune more if the plant grows out of bounds at any time. Hardy geranium are susceptible to relatively few pests or diseases; however, if watered heavily from the top of the plant in shadier conditions, they can develop powdery mildew and fungal problems. If that happens to your geraniums, cut off infected leaves, but do not compost; be sure to throw the infected leaves away.

37

GROW A BUTTERFLY FLOWER:
HOW ABOUT BUTTERFLY WEED?
Monarchs love this native bloomer

SMOTHERED WITH BUTTERFLIES throughout summer, butterfly weed or *Asclepias tuberosa* is a good-looking, sweet-scented plant that attracts beneficial insects of all sorts. It's a relative to the common milkweed, but does not have the sticky sap associated with the taller plant. It can be a rather impactful plant in the organic home garden. Hack a garden filled with butterflies by planting butterfly weed in your garden and help the movement to save the monarchs.

Butterfly weed is native to many parts of North America. If placed in full sun, its bold orange-red flowers can bloom continuously until the first frost. Hummingbirds love the flowers, but deer and other pests will typically not eat it. Happily, butterfly weed will grow in most any soil and truly prefers poor soil to rich. Do not plant in areas where water is likely to pool; the native can handle some moisture, but really needs a well-drained bed. Amend soil to create proper drainage if necessary. Start either from potted plants or seed. Butterfly weed seed performs significantly better when exposed to up to six weeks of winter conditions before they will produce growth and can take up to three years to develop flowers.

Plant this flower in its permanent location because its long taproot is not easily dug up; if you dig up the plant and the taproot breaks, the plant will die. Deadheading helps give more abundant flower production, but is not necessary. There are no regular insect or disease issues. Keep in mind that this plant is considered poisonous; in fact, insects eat the toxins within the nectar and become toxic and distasteful to their natural predators. Be sure small children

WHAT'S GOING ON WITH MONARCHS?
Recent statistics released by the World Wildlife Fund show that the numbers of monarch butterflies are declining. With milkweed being replaced by genetically modified crops and urban population centers, it is becoming more difficult for the monarchs to find a healthy migration zone. Common milkweed is their favorite food, but butterfly weed is another plant in the *Asclepias* genus that can help.

^ Butterfly weed produces beautifully fragrant, nectar-filled orange flowers and is most commonly found in the native plant section of local garden centers.

and animals do not touch or eat the plants as these toxins can harm mammals. New butterfly weed plants may benefit from a weekly watering until the taproot is well established. After that, only water if there is an ongoing drought.

^ Bees need a source of water in their
pollination territory. Providing a floating bee
preserver enables the bee to have a drink
without drowning in deeper pools of water.
*Photo credit: Robin Haglund/Garden
Mentors® of www.gardenmentors.com.
Glass artist: Barbara Sanderson of
www.glassgardensNW.com.*

AN IDEA WORTH FLOATING:
BEE PRESERVERS
You can lead a bee to water and help it drink

WITH BEE POPULATIONS down and so much concern about colony collapse, it is important for every gardener to do his or her part to help the bees. Planting native and flowering plants is a start. Many insects get water from their food, but bees need to drink an ample quantity of pure water. And water can be hard for bees to access: many sources such as ponds, lakes, and rivers do not have a landing area for bees, and they can drown in deeper water.

Building a bee station to help the bees have regular access to water is as simple as using a birdbath and a bee preserver. Bee preservers are wonderful glass balls with bumps on them that float on top of a water source and allow bees to crawl to the water without drowning. Fill the bath with water and add about 10 to 12 drops of lemongrass oil, an essential oil that will attract bees and that you can find in many health food stores. A bee's sense of smell is powerful, and the lemongrass oil is similar to a pheromone that honeybees use to attract a swarm to a new home. If you would prefer not to attract honeybees to your garden and just want to provide an open source of water for pollinators of all kinds, be sure to regularly freshen water in birdbaths or other water garden areas where a bee preserver might float. Fresh water is essential for bees.

If standing water and the possibility of increasing mosquito production is a concern for your community, try floating wine corks or chopped up sticks on the top of a bucket or birdbath filled with water. Another idea is to fill a birdbath with river stone, then cover the river stone with just enough water that little pockets of liquid can be accessed by the bees. Clean the water regularly and watch both pollinating bees and wasps come in for a sip. They will visit at all times during the day, but make a concentrated effort at drinking toward late afternoon and early evening.

THIS IS IMPORTANT:
SAVE THE BEES
Home gardeners can take a lead role in rebuilding bee habitat

BEES ARE IMPORTANT to humanity for a very crucial reason; our food supply can be compromised without the bee population. Bees are responsible for pollinating everything from strawberries to citrus, vegetables, nuts, seeds, and onions. Even dairy products are a part of a detailed food chain that starts with bee pollination. According to *U.S. News & World Report*:

> The U.S. Department of Agriculture considers annual [bee] colony losses above 19 percent to be economically unsustainable. Yet, a full two-thirds of American beekeepers are suffering loses at more than double that threshold [in 2015]. If this loss rate continues to rise, beekeepers will be forced out of business—and supermarkets could soon follow.

Which means, in no uncertain terms, we must change our ways to help save the bees. Growers in home gardens and big agriculture alike must stop using pesticides. The challenge begins at home: The best thing to do is start planting more pollinating plants organically—without chemical fertilizers, pesticides, and herbicides—no matter if you live in a small apartment with a balcony or on a large farm. Support local organically grown produce and honey in order to help local beekeepers in your area. Honey bees are just the beginning: there are more than 4,000 species of native or wild bees in the United States.

Plant wildflowers and native plants that support the local bee population. In order to discover what these plants might be, consult with your local extension office or independent garden center. When planting annual flowers, stay away from plants that might not attract bees and instead focus on pollinator plants for your garden. DO NOT use pesticides, herbicides, or other chemicals in your garden. Let herbs and other plants bolt (go to flower). Provide a fresh water source.

BEE-ATTRACTING PLANTS

- Alyssum
- Agastache
- Asclepias
- Asters
- Borage
- Chives
- Clover
- Coneflowers
- Cornflower
- Cosmos
- Fennel
- Goldenrod
- Japanese Anemone
- Lavender
- Mint
- Monarda
- Oregano
- Sunflower
- Verbena
- Zinnia

< Coneflowers are a wonderful perennial to help attract bees to your garden. Bees love exploring the base of the coneflowers. Find coneflowers that are native to your region or gorgeous hybrids at your local garden center.

WHEN HERBS BOLT, LET THEM GO
Pollinators love the flowers

∧ Let your herbs bolt so bees and other pollinators can enjoy your herbs all season long. This bee is supping from *Thymus pulegioides* 'Foxley'. *Photo credit: Robin Haglund/Garden Mentors® of www.gardenmentors.com.*

MOTHER NATURE HAS designed herbs to reproduce. This means that the act of flowering and producing seeds is each plant's ultimate goal. All herbs eventually bolt: The plant changes from being mostly leaf-based to a plant that has mostly flowers and stems. Bolting typically raises the stem and flower above the herbal base. You will recognize a bolted plant because it will be happily flowering. When this happens, the herb itself loses flavor, making it basically inedible, as it is putting all its energy into creating seed.

In order to enjoy the fresh flavor of your herbs a bit longer, you should plant them tightly and keep them well-watered. Cooling the roots with an insulating layer of mulch helps stave off the heat. Still, once the weather turns hot and dry, your herbs will bolt rapidly, going from delicious to inedible sometimes in a matter of hours. So keeping the plant cooler will assist in preserving flavor by delaying the bolting. When you can no longer keep your herbs from bolting, let them bolt hard. That is, let them fully develop their flowers so bees and other pollinators can enjoy the flower nectar. In order to continue enjoying flavorful herbs, install another row or grouping of herbs. Succession planting can keep you in delicious scents and flavors all season long, while also enabling the pollinators to stay happy and healthy.

TIP: Harvest your herbs directly from the top of your plant as often as possible as you will be snipping off immature flower buds before they develop.

∧ The herbs pollinators prefer include basil, bee balm, betony, borage, catmint, chives, fennel, hyssop, lavender, lemon balm, marjoram, mint, oregano, sage, and rosemary. Start your first crop of herbs in winter from seed, plant the young plants in the early spring, then succession-plant seeds next to the first crop once it is in ground. As the first crop starts to bolt, the second crop will start with its first fresh leafy flavors. Invasive crops such as mint and oregano can be contained by planting them in containers.' *Photo credit: Alexander Raths/Shutterstock*

HACK A HOME FOR MASON BEES

They are fantastic pollinators for your garden

NATIVE BEES IN the United States have had significant population losses, but are holding out as a bit heartier than honey bees. They have an independent, non-social nature, and they do not make commercial honey. But you should get to know mason bees. They are a gentle, nest-building native bees that do not sting and are amazing pollinators. There are around 140 species of mason bee that live in North America. Typically, mason bees are active for 8 to 10 weeks in the spring, then go dormant and hibernate for 10 months until their next pollinating adventure.

If your garden does not have enough pollen and nectar for mason bees, they will move on. Planting a diverse, blooming, 300-foot circle of spring-flowering plants around a mason bee house will help the bees survive and stay in your garden. Native plants are the best for native bees, according to The Xerces Society. Mason bees will emerge about the time the redbud trees bloom in your region, with populations at all-time highs during apple-blossom season. One bee can pollinate more than 1,500 blossoms per day, which makes these bees vital in orchards.

Plant your gardens with no chemical fertilizers or pesticides to encourage the health of all bees, and grow early flowering plants and shrubs such as forsythia, crocus, primrose, snowdrops, Lenten rose, and pulmonaria to feed them. To extend their season by a few weeks and encourage the bees to hang on a little longer, plant sweet-scented roses, forget-me-nots, cranesbill geranium, borage, comfrey, sweetpea, penstemon, salvia, and allium. Also provide mud for your bees so they can use it to build their homes—

∧ Place a mason bee housing near a patio so you can watch these gentle creatures coming and going throughout the day on their pollinating adventures.

purchase it online, or simply fill a tub or trench with muddy soil for the bees.

Mason bee houses are easy to find. They consist of a collection of long empty tubes or reeds surrounded by some sort of housing. The bees live in the tubes. You can make your own nesting boxes by drilling 20 or 30 holes in a non-treated block of wood. Use a very sharp drill bit so there are no splinters, and drill $5/16$-inch holes, 6 inches deep in the block. Mount your nesting house at least 3 feet above the ground, tight to a fence, tree, or building protected from rain, and with full warm sun in the morning. Remove the wooden block houses every two years and retire them in order to protect the bees from possible disease problems.

SEED and SEEDLING hacks

HACKS IN THIS CHAPTER

GIVE SEEDS A SOAK TO HELP THEM SPROUT
Sometimes a little scratching helps too

SEEDS, WHEN LEFT to their own devices, will stratify over winter on the ground, or perhaps will be swallowed by a bird or squirrel and returned to the soil later. These processes help crack the seeds' hard exterior shells so that a new plant can emerge in the spring. Soaking seeds before planting can help emulate that process, breaking down the seeds' hard exterior, which will better enable sprouting.

When seeds are particularly large or have thicker exteriors, they can be helped along in the germination process by being scarified. Seed scarification means sanding, nicking, or chipping off a bit of the seed's shell so that water can be absorbed by the interior of the seed and so begin the germination process. Cracking or scratching a seed's coating is much easier to do with larger seeds; smaller seeds can be crushed when scarified, so care needs to be taken in the process.

Large or thick seeds should be scarified, then soaked in a small cup of warm water overnight. They will be ready to plant when the seeds have swollen and lightened slightly in color. To soak smaller seeds, there is no need to scarify: simply place the small seeds on a paper towel and gently drench with water. Let soak between 3 and 12 hours, checking regularly to see if the seed swells. Do not soak seeds too long as they can become too heavily drenched with water and disintegrate.

∧ Soaking seeds will help loosen the seed materials from their husks so that a new sprout can emerge and grow.
Photo credit: Crystal Liepa

Warm water is more effective when soaking seeds than cold water, but hot water can kill seeds. Soaking the seeds in manure tea (see Hack 18: "Brew a Batch of Manure Tea") is a common practice, although fertilizer is not required for seed starting.

43

PET TENDER SEEDLINGS
TO KEEP THEM STRONG & STOCKY
Put thigmotropism to work for you

PETTING YOUR SEEDLINGS can help them grow stockier, healthier stems. Thigmotropism or the thigmo-response is a fancy term that describes how a plant bends or turns in response to a particular touch stimulus. There are many examples of this in the garden; for example, when a sweet pea or wisteria vine's tendrils touch a solid object, it causes a coiling response that causes the plant to curl around the object. It "feels" the support and bends in reaction to the shared touch because of specific hormones that function as chemical messengers within the plant or seedling. Plants respond in many ways to a touch stimulus, and seedlings have a unique reaction.

Seedlings are particularly responsive to touch stimulus. They can also suffer from lack of light when started indoors during winter. Many seedlings grow leggy even with grow light assistance. Touch stimulus helps keep the plant short and stocky, which in turn helps the plants grow at a rate that works better for starting indoors. Additionally, this type of stimulation can affect the plant throughout its life, not just as a seedling.

Simply brush your hand over the tops of your seedlings every day or every other day, barely caressing them. Leaves and growing tips of the plants will be the most affected, so ignore the stems and focus on the very tips and leaf structure. Because wind has a similar effect to a gentle caress, it has been theorized that setting up a fan near your seedlings also help them to grow stronger. Also, the extra air movement will help prevent fungal issues for the seedlings.

< Pet your seedlings by running your hands over their tops to help them become stronger and have healthier stems.

44

MAKE A MINI-NURSERY

A clever hack for rotisserie chicken containers

THE COST OF purchasing seedlings can add up quickly. Instead of putting a dent in your financials to start plants, why not reuse rotisserie chicken containers as mini-nurseries for seed starting? Costco alone sells more than 60 million rotisserie chickens per year. Rotisserie chicken containers are food-safe, great for indoor seed starting because of their small size, and have a built-in nursery cover. A cost advantage of using rotisserie chicken containers once the chicken has been removed is that they are also free for you to reuse for a quick planting project.

One thing these containers do not have is drain holes. So there are two methods of seed starting you can choose from, depending on the space you have available. The best bet is to punch a few small holes in the bottom of the containers for drainage, then set them on top of rimmed cookie sheets for the growing process. Drainage will be controlled because the cookie sheets will catch any liquid. If you prefer to not punch holes in the bottom of the container, then you must be very careful to not overwater your seedlings. Overwatering can cause damping-off conditions. One advantage of not punching holes in your container is that you can then set the container directly on a heating vent or over a heating pad to promote sprouting.

> Before planting seedlings, make sure the soil is finely sifted without lumps. Use a fork to break up any lumps in the soil you may have.

< Grow seeds from a reliable seed company, following the directions on the package when planting.

> Seeds can be large or very tiny. Smaller seeds usually require light to germinate, so must be planted on top of the soil, not buried below.

< Start your seeds about six to eight weeks before it's time to plant them in the ground. Place your planting container in a warm area near a sunny window to optimize light for the seedlings.

< Seedlings soon sprout up in the miniature greenhouse.

Fill the bottom of the container with seed-starting mix or organic soil, and add water before you plant the seeds. Following the directions on your seed packet, gently poke holes in the soil if the seeds require dark to germinate, or sprinkle the seeds on the top of the soil if they require light to germinate. Cover with your clear rotisserie container lid and keep a close eye on the growing seedlings. Place beneath grow lights or in a sunny window. Soil should remain moist during sprouting. Once seeds have sprouted, ventilate the container regularly to prevent fungal growth or damping-off conditions. Once the seedlings get larger, be sure to remove the lid and let the plants get plenty of light and fresh air.

45

GIVE INDOOR STARTS
A SLOW INTRODUCTION TO THE GARDEN
It's a hard world outside for seedlings

WHEN SEEDLINGS ARE started indoors over the winter, they are living a pampered life filled with love: warm, controlled temperatures; regular water; and consistent light exposure. Plants tend to thrive in these conditions, but the hospitable environment can also allow them to become a bit spoiled and delicate. Hardening-off your seedlings enables your plants to toughen up a bit before they are faced with harsh, sometimes windy, sometimes cold, and sometimes hot environments. Hardening-off your seedlings is a simple hack that will help prepare your babies for the real world experience of living outdoors in all types of weather. Soon they will get used to heavy rains, cold nights, and outlandishly hot afternoons. Until then, continue to keep your plants evenly moist during the hardening-off process. Take your seedlings out to a protected area that gets light, but not scorching sun. Bring the seedlings out for one or two hours per day the first few days then gradually increase their exposure to the sun. Pay special attention to the plants and make sure they do not wilt. Increase exposure by an hour a day for 7 to 10 days. By the end of that time the babies will be pre-teens and ready for the soil.

As an example, hardy plants such as winter vegetables, early spring vegetables, and perennials can be brought out regularly in 40°F (4°C). Tender plants such as delicate annual flowers, coleus, herbs, cucumber, pumpkin, tomatoes, peppers, and squash should be brought out after 50° to 60°F (10° to 16°C).

∧ Hardening-off your seedlings is the process of getting your plant babies acclimated to the outdoor environment. Simply planting your seedlings directly without the hardening-off process can kill them. Slowly introducing the plants to the outdoors can help them grow stronger before planting.

When planting in the ground or in containers, be sure to put the recommended amount of organic fertilizer in the planting soil in order to give the new plant a positive boost for the roots. Continue to keep the plants evenly moist until you see the plants truly take hold in the new environment. This will help your plants avoid transplant shock and have a healthier beginning in their new home.

A HACK FOR HARVESTING TOMATO SEED BOUNTY

Squish them, dry them, and plant them—all on a paper towel

COLLECTING AND PROPAGATING seed at home can be a tremendously rewarding experience. Propagating a new plant from the seeds of a fruit or vegetable that you have grown yourself is easy to do if you have the right type of plant. Although most plants produce seeds, some modern hybridized plants are not able to reproduce from seed and will not germinate well in the garden. For other plants, you are not legally allowed propagate their seeds at home because the plants are patented. Still other plants do not grow true when grown from seed: their offspring will not resemble the original fruit or vegetable. For plants that you can propagate—legally and vegetatively—here is an amazing way to hack free seeds from the garden.

> In order to save cherry tomato seeds from the previous season, simply squish the tomatoes in an unbleached paper napkin or towel, dry, cut into squares, and save for the next season. Plant directly in potting soil in the spring.

^ Lay cherry tomatoes out on an open, unbleached napkin or paper towel.

^ Squish the tomatoes, remove any large tomato chunks, and leave the seeds.

HOW TO USE PAPER TOWELS TO SEED-SAVE

(using cherry tomatoes as an example)

1. Collect cherry tomatoes fresh from the garden.
2. Place one tomato inside an unbleached paper towel or napkin.
3. Squish the paper towel and tomato flat, letting the seeds spread apart within the paper.
4. Open up the towel and gently pull out any very large chunks, then fold closed again.
5. Let the tomato seeds and towel dry completely. A good way to do this is to lay out the flattened tomato and towel on top of your clothes dryer.
6. When dry, cut the tomato seed paper into squares.
7. Store over the winter in a paper bag, which allows for air circulation.
8. In the spring, at the proper time for your area, plant the paper towel squares directly in the garden or in a starting container, about a ¼ inch below the surface of the soil.
9. Water well with a diluted liquid organic fertilizer and water mixture.
10. Once seedlings get several inches high, transplant into a permanent location.

MIX UP A BATCH OF SEED-STARTER SOIL
Loose soil helps the baby seeds jump into the world

STARTING YOUR OWN seeds at home is easier when you hack a starter mix that helps the seeds grow to their full potential. Healthy seedlings need a loose, well-drained medium made of fine particles of organic material. Potting soil can be used, but it usually doesn't drain as well as a finer seed starting mix.

Ken Druse, author of *Making More Plants: The Science, Art and Joy of Propagation* and garden podcaster from "Ken Druse Real Dirt," has a marvelous recipe for making a homemade seed starting mix. It works very well as a light, airy, and sound starting mix for your seedlings. Here is his special recipe.

∧ Once you hack your homemade seed-starting soil mix, fill the seed-starting containers before planting the seeds.

KEN'S HOMEMADE SEED-STARTING SOIL MIX

1. Start with homemade leaf mold (see Hack 3: "Seek Out Free Mulch") that has been sieved through a ½-inch hardware cloth screen so only the smallest bits of the leaf mold remain.
2. Mix 4 parts screened leaf mold with 1 part perlite and 1 part chicken grit.
3. Moisten the mix and place in a large roasting bag, shake up, close the top loosely with the non-metal tie that comes with the bag or a string.
4. Sterilize the leaf mold by microwaving for 10 minutes on full power.
5. Take the temperature of the leaf mold mixture by opening the bag—be careful as the steam is hot—it should be at 180°F or 82.22°C. Let your starting mix cool.
6. Place this sowing medium in containers, then sow the seeds.

Following the directions on the seed packet, tiny seeds are barely covered; larger ones are buried to a depth equal to their thickness. Until the seedlings develop, do not let the seed-starting mix dry completely. Add water to a tray beneath the pots to let them soak up moisture, or gently spray pots with water from a sprayer. Most seeds need light to germinate. Some seedlings will appear in only a week, while others take several weeks or longer. The seed packets should have this specific information.

HACK YOUR OWN DIY SEED TAPE
A little TP goes a long way when planting in rows

WHY BUY SEED-PLANTING tapes when you can hack them on your own? Making seed tapes during the winter months, then storing them for when you are ready to plant takes out the challenges of spacing seeds properly and can eliminate thinning later. Plant your seed tape based on the final, post-thinning seedling measurements for a time- and money-saving planting tool.

SUPPLIES NEEDED
- Biodegradable unbleached toilet paper
- 3 tablespoons unbleached flour
- 1.5 tablespoons water
- Toothpick
- Small spoon
- Pen
- Ruler or yardstick
- Seeds—save the seed packets

> Biodegradable seed tapes are easy to plant and simple to make with toilet paper and your favorite seeds.

HOW TO MAKE BIODEGRADABLE SEED TAPE

1. Pull off several feet of the toilet paper.
2. Fold the toilet paper in half length-wise. Run your hand down the edge to make the fold crisp.
3. Pour the seeds out of the seed packet and separate them on a plate.
4. Read the packet and make sure you understand how far apart you should place the seeds in the ground based on the post-thinning distance.
5. Mix the flour and water together to make a thick natural glue—if it is too thin, just thicken it up with a bit more flour.
6. Open the toilet paper sheet up and place a ruler or yardstick next to the sheet.
7. Dip a toothpick into the glue paste to pick up a healthy drop.
8. Touch the toothpick with the flour paste on to one seed.
9. Pick up the seed and gently place it onto the middle of the toilet paper every few inches as the seed packet directs.
10. Once you have placed the seeds on the entire length of the paper, use a small spoon and place a bit of the glue along the edge of the toilet paper, refold the paper, and seal it.
11. Continue until you have made enough seed tape to plant your garden design.
12. Write the name of the plant and suggested planting depth on the bottom edge of the seed strip, then roll the strip up carefully and store within a sealed container in a cool, dry spot.
13. At planting time, simply dig a small trench in your garden bed or container garden based on the seed packet instructions and unroll the seed packet along the trench.
14. Cover with soil and water well.

ʌ Using the flour and water mixture, place drops of the mixture at measured intervals along the strip, then place a single seed in each drop.

ʌ Simply lay the folded strip along the soil, cover gently, and water, then wait for your seeds to grow into seedlings.

A PICTURE-PERFECT HACK FOR STORING SEEDS

Organize your seed packets in photo albums

GARDENERS OFTEN DROWN in all their seed packets, often tossed in an old drawer or thrown in a paper bag for safekeeping—the confusion becomes nearly impossible to sort through. Without a safe storage area, seeds can suffer from fungal problems related to moisture growth within the seed packet. While glass jars, small baggies filled with desiccant, and cardboard boxes do work, they sometimes become challenging to sort. Special plastic boxes such as the Seed Keeper Kit from The Seed Keeper Company also works well because it includes alphabetic divider cards for the seeds. However, to hack your own homemade seed organizer, try using a photo album with special pocket pages.

Using a photo album allows you to store more than one seed packet per pocket. It is also easy to include other garden information such as plastic plant labels or seed trade lists. Pages can be rearranged in the book as needed to help you better organize. This allows for better alphabetizing or categorizing according to plant type, such as flowers, brassicas, roots, legumes, ornamental edibles, herbs, or perennials.

There are two categories of seed packet saving—seed-filled packets or empty, used seed packets. Saving either can be important to your garden. How many times have you planted a garden container or bed and realized you did not

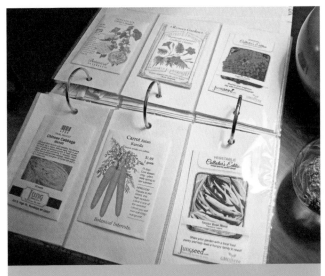

∧ Simply use a photo album to organize and save seed packets for easy access and reference.

know how far apart to thin the seedlings? By saving your seed packets as reference material, you can look back and better answer any questions you might have about the plants.

Another idea for seed packet storage is to store your seeds by planting date. Tuck pieces of paper in each photo album page pocket with the planting date and location in your garden where the seeds should be planted. This will help you hack the upcoming growing season with ease.

BLOOMING hacks

HACKS IN THIS CHAPTER

50

GO SOAK YOUR BULBS

A short bath before planting time encourages germination

FLOWERING BULBS ARE a true delight in the home and garden. You can help give your bulbs a nice start by soaking them in manure tea. But soaking your bulbs for too long can be disastrous as it can trigger fungal problems, so keep an eye on the bulbs during the soaking process to make sure there are no complications.

- **For flowering bulbs** Soak bulbs—both spring- and fall-flowering bulbs—in the manure tea for 24 hours. Add organic fertilizer to the soil as recommended by the grower at planting time, then drench the soil with the remaining manure tea after planting in the ground.
- **For amaryllis and paperwhite bulbs** These winter bulbs, particularly amaryllis, typically like it dry. Soak them for 30 minutes in the manure tea. Paperwhite bulbs can go longer, but not more than 24 hours. Water the plants with the manure tea once every two weeks.
- **For vegetable bulbs** Planting bulbs and stem vegetables in the same location every season can deplete your garden soil. Crop rotation is key, but so is soil amendment throughout the seasons. Bulbs and stem crops such as garlic, onions, asparagus, cardoon, celeriac, fennel, kohlrabi, leeks, shallots, and chives can also benefit from a soaking with the manure tea 24 hours before planting.

HOW TO SOAK BULBS

1. Mix up a batch of full-strength manure tea (see Hack 18: "Brew a Batch of Manure Tea").
2. Soak the bulbs in the manure tea for the recommended length of time (see left).
3. Plant as directed.
4. Drench the planting area with the remaining manure tea.

∧ Soaking bulbs in a manure tea mixture can help give the bulbs an extra energy boost before planting.

51

OUTFIT YOUR SEEDLINGS WITH A ONE-GALLON HAT
A milk jug cloche protects your tender plants

TRADITIONAL CLOCHES AND BELL JARS have been used in gardening since the 1800s. French market gardeners were known to use the glass cloches as miniature greenhouses to help extend their spring and fall plantings. This made it possible to grow and support "out of season" herbs and vegetables for a longer period of time.

While classic glass bell jars are still available, they are made from remarkably heavy glass. This glass can function like a magnifying glass, focusing heat from the sun inside the cloche. Because cloches are usually quite small, the intense heat inside can kill plants. This makes ventilation critical. A milk jug cloche makes that ventilation simple.

In order to hack your own inexpensive cloche to help extend your planting season, simply cut the bottom of a plastic milk jug and set the jug directly over a plant that needs a little extended help. Remove the cap of the milk

∧ Using a milk jug as a cloche is an inexpensive way to hack a longer growing season; it protects plants and so extends production.

jug for ventilation; if additional airflow is needed, you can prop the side up with a stick or piece of wood. Since the milk jug is not made out of heavy glass, there is less heat generated. Keep in mind, however, that without as much heat generation, the system does not provide as much heavy frost protection.

Keep an eye on your plants as cloches can also hold moisture in if they are not ventilated often enough. This moisture can help the plant in some cases, but it can also encourage fungal problems.

52

A CHEAP AND EASY WAY TO MAKE A BED

Everyday items only; no power tools required

DO YOU WANT an organic raised garden bed that does not rely on chemically treated wood and is as easy to remove as it is to build? No worries! Simply hack a raised bed with old fencing, straw, and your favorite soil mix.

The first step is finding a raised bed site location. Have the soil tested below the bed to determine if your raised bed garden should be planted with or without a ground barrier. Additional concerns for a barrier might be considered if you are worried about ground rodents. For instance, if you have gophers or moles in your planting area, it might be beneficial to put your soil in after adding a layer of hardware cloth.

> These raised beds are easy to hack together in your garden. They are temporary but hold soil and plant roots firmly in place.

HOW TO BUILD A RAISED BED

1. Decide whether or not to lay a hardware cloth barrier (see previous page).
2. You will be creating a round garden. Determine what the diameter of the garden will be. Drive a stake in the ground in the precise center of your planned raised bed garden site.
3. Tie a rope the length of the radius to the stake and use it as a trammel and lay out the circle. Mark the circle's perimeter with a garden hose.
4. Use a hoe or shovel to dig a narrow trench around the perimeter and remove grass and weeds that might be inside the perimeter.
5. Bury the fencing so 6 to 8 inches of fence projects above ground.
6. Rake the soil in the bed site so it is flat and level.
7. Install optional hardware cloth, using wire cutters to custom-fit the cloth to the space.
8. Line the inside of the fencing with loose straw or grass clippings, back fill with planting soil to help hold the straw up along the fencing.
9. Fill the raised garden bed with organic soil to just below the top of the fence. An excellent homemade soil mix is 1 part organic potting soil with worm castings, 1 part organic rotted composted manure, and 1 part plain compost or leaf mold.
10. Rake the soil flat.
11. Plant the garden.

SUPPLIES NEEDED
- Stake
- Hammer
- Rope or string
- Hoe or shovel
- Heavy gauge wire garden fencing cut 8 to 12 inches high
- Wire cutters
- Straw or grass clippings
- Garden hose
- Rake
- Hardware cloth (optional)

This raised bed gardening hack is perfect if you have some old straw or grass clippings and a bit of garden fencing left from a previous project. Because the sides of the raised beds are open, it is possible for the roots to get more aeration. You gain a temporary seasonal garden that is easy to clean up at the end of the growing year.

53

CHEAP TRICKS FOR MANAGING WEEDS
Keep control without reaching for chemical herbicides

WEED CONTROL IS always a challenge. Pulling weeds out by the roots is the best way to eliminate them in an organic garden. It gets the job done with no chemicals and no drama. Yet with our busy lives filled with too much work and not enough relaxation, staying on top of the weeds is difficult, and it doesn't take long at all for the weeds to get out of control. Below are a few quick garden hacks for eliminating weeds without heavy chemicals.

HOW TO MANAGE WEEDS

- **Tools** Using the proper tool for the weeding job is important. Tap roots do not come out easily with a shallow digging tool, so using a hori hori knife or a dandelion puller for weeds with taproots make sense. Weeds that grow in the gaps around brick pavers or flagstones can be dug out with a narrow, pointy tool such as a crack weeder or claw weeder.

- **Vinegar** Fill a spray bottle with 3 parts white vinegar to 1 part natural castile soap, and gently mix them. Spray on weeds in a narrow stream. This will kill the top of the plants, but might not get a long taproot permanently. For a more potent vinegar solution that kills weeds to the bottom of the root, use a horticultural-grade vinegar, which is much stronger.

- **Salt** Salt is best used in an area where you do not want other plants to grow again, such as along a flagstone path, in between sidewalk cracks, or on your driveway. Before an expected rain, pour generic table salt onto the weeds. As soon as the weeds are moistened with a bit of rainwater, the salt will soak down into the soil, killing the weedy plants.

- **Boiling water** For a 100-percent natural, safe, and inexpensive solution, try boiling water, which kills weed seeds and plants immediately. Very slowly and carefully pour boiling water over weeds and weed seeds. Proceed slowly so you don't burn yourself.

< Weed control in sidewalk and driveway cracks is easy with generic table salt; simply pour the salt on the weeds before a rainfall.

54

MULCH YOUR GARDENS WITH GREEN
A living groundcover works hard and looks great

PLANTING A LIVING MULCH offers many benefits to your perennial gardens. Have a difficult area where weeds grow? You have mulched the spot, but weed control has been inadequate even with a heavy layer of mulch? This is the perfect location to hack a living mulch using groundcovers or low-growing shrubs.

Groundcovers do not typically need high levels of water or sun—there are exceptions to this, of course—but those with lower sun and moisture requirements can help a garden use less water and be more sustainable while keeping weeds at bay. Groundcovers are amazing plants to help prevent soil erosion, especially on sloping ground. Groundcovers used as living mulch help protect the soil from extreme temperatures. Leaf drop through the fall and winter helps add microbes to the soil beneath the plants.

While groundcovers can function in full shade, even the plants that adore shade need a little filtered sunlight or early morning sun. Groundcovers that work well in dry shady areas include ajuga, bergenia, periwinkle, sweet woodruff, creeping thyme, Christmas fern, Solomon's seal, hellebore, lamium,

pachysandra, Korean boxwood, yew, and Spanish bluebell. Also consider native plants for your region.

Sun-loving groundcovers that function well in a hot, sunny location include sedum, moss phlox, snow-in-summer, nepeta, lavender, thyme, delosperma, daylily, coreopsis, hen and chicks, and lamb's ears. Shrubs that make excellent sunny groundcovers include cotoneaster, clethra, dwarf fothergilla, Virginia sweetspire, and Knock Out® roses. Consider native shrubs first as they require the least amount of work and attract native wildlife.

Since you know that your groundcovers will be in the same location in the garden for a long time, prepare the soil well. Follow the tag's planting directions; make sure that the soil is amended with organic matter that allows for drainage so the plants are not standing in water.

< This lovely woodland garden shows layers of groundcovers and groundcover plantings being used as mulch cover for the soil surface.

55

HOST AN ALLIUM FAMILY RE-ONION
Use these flowering bulbs in dry arrangements

ALLIUMS ARE A GENUS of bulbous flowering plants that are related to the onion. Most varieties, such as garlic, chives, leek, and flowering alliums, are pest resistant and easy to grow. What makes alliums so unique and wonderful is their tendency to have round, flowering heads that look equally marvelous in the garden or in a flower arrangement. Freshly cut flowers last a long time in water, and when they eventually dry, they retain their globe form, extending their lives long enough for you to hack a creative craft or flower arrangement utilizing their flower heads. Here are lists of rounded-form Allium flowering varieties.

HOW TO DRY ALLIUMS

1. Cut allium stems at the base of the plant down by the basal leaves. Do not cut the leaves or pull them out; leave them to dry so they might continue to provide energy for the bulb for next season.
2. Place the cut flowers in 2 inches of fresh water, preferably in a tall vase to help support the stem.
3. Place the vase out of direct sunlight for two weeks or until all the water is absorbed and the flowers turn a golden brown.
4. You can also cut already-dried stems directly out of the garden, but they are more likely to bend or break if dried in-field versus dried utilizing the water-and-vase technique.

Some gardeners choose to paint the dried heads as they stand in the garden, but a more practical outlook is to collect the drying flowers by cutting them at the base of their stem. Once the flowers are completely dry, it is easy to paint them or spray them with food coloring for interesting effect.

Large-balled Allium varieties

Allium aflatunense 'Purple Sensation'

A. Ambassador

A. *christophii* (Star of Persia)

A. 'Globemaster'

A. 'Gladiator'

A. *karataviense*

A. 'Mount Everest'

A. 'Pinball Wizard'

A. *stipitatum* 'White Giant'

A. *schubertii*

Small- to medium-balled Allium varieties

Allium amplectens 'Graceful Beauty'

A. *atropurpureum*

A. *azureum*

A. *sphaerocephalon* 'Drumstick'

A. *flavum*

A. 'Forelock'

A. *vineale* 'Hair'

< Alliums have a unique ball form and offer a lot of creative potential for reuse in flower arrangements and crafts.

< Once the allium flowers
have bloomed, then
seed heads form. These
seedheads can be painted
and reused in craft and
flower arrangements.
*Photo credit: Stacy
of OliveLoaf Design at
www.oliveloafdesign.
wordpress.com.*

∧ Flower heads are
beautiful in flower
arrangements. Should the
stems droop, use a strong
floral wire to help support
the allium head.

PLANT BEE-FRIENDLY PERENNIALS
THAT STAND UP TO DROUGHT
Conserve water and help pollinators: a win/win hack

DO YOU WANT to save money by watering less, but still have a beautiful garden that needs very little attention? Try planting a drought-tolerant or native perennial garden this season. It is a great way to hack the drought and help the bees at the same time. Native plants are always a better choice to attract local pollinators, and the perennials listed below are hardy common perennials that are easily found in garden centers. Most of these plants tolerate tough planting conditions and have lower water needs, and almost all of them are ornamental for much of the growing season and so attract pollinating insects over a long period of time.

Keep in mind that all plants need more water their first season to get established. Amend your planting area with natural and organic soil amendments, then follow the guides on the plant tags for planting needs. In order to better support a perennial garden, water less frequently but more deeply. A heavy soak of the garden at the root level during establishment ensures a deeper and better developed root system as well as fewer fungus issues on the top of the plant.

DROUGHT-TOLERANT, BEE-ATTRACTING PERENNIALS

- Yarrow   (*Achillea*)
- Stonecrop   (*Sedum*) all varieties
- Russian sage   (*Perovskia atriplicifolia*)
- Penstemon   (*Penstemon*) all varieties
- Lamb's ears   (*Stachys byzantine*)
- Gayfeather   (*Liatris*)
- Coreopsis   (*Coreopsis*) all varieties
- Coneflower   (*Echinacea*) all varieties
- Goldenrod   (*Solidago*) all varieties
- Lavender   (*Lavandula*) all varieties

> Bees love native plants like gayfeather and coneflower best. Plant as many drought-tolerant, full-season flowering, low-maintenance plants as you can to attract both native bees and honey bees to your community.

A SIMPLE HACK FOR COLLECTING SEEDS
Paper bags are a true labor saver

SEED COLLECTING IS easiest after the flowers and plants in your garden have ripened for the season. While there are many complicated ways to capture seeds from seedheads, the easiest hack is the good old paper bag method. This method allows you to capture the seed at just the right time. When you pick the seeds too early, the seed does not always survive the drying process; if you wait too long, the seed may have already dropped or blown away.

In order to collect seed with the bag method, it is important that you target healthy plants with abundant ripe seedheads. When most of the seedheads turn from green to a shade of brown, it means they are drying on the stem. Choose a plant that does not have fungal problems and still has healthy seedpods.

Put a paper bag over the selected plant's dried seedheads, then tie the bag closed with a string or rubber band so that the seeds cannot easily escape. Then snip the stem off at the top of the bag and turn the bag right side up. Label the bag with the plant/seed name, then store the bag in a very clean and dry location for several days or months; do not freeze. The best temperature is approximately 40° to 50°F (5 to 10°C). Do not store wet material—only clean and dry seeds inside a dry bag.

Open the paper bag and shake the stems before removing them from the bag to collect the seed. Remove the seeds and store in paper bags or envelopes; avoid plastic bags or airtight containers unless the seeds are thoroughly dried before storage.

< Collecting seeds from the garden is easy to do with a brown paper bag, rubber band or string, and a pair of snippers.

Other seed collections tips

- Do not collect seeds that have been on the ground for a length of time because you might not be collecting the correct varieties.
- Fleshy, wet fruits such as squash or tomatoes need to be collected off the plant. Then the seeds should be removed, washed, and dried in the open because they can become hot, moldy, and rot in an enclosed moist area. Seek seeds that are fully ripe, hard, and darker in color, not green or soft.

EDIBLES
hacks

HACKS IN THIS CHAPTER

58

HELP HERBS AND VEGETABLES
SURVIVE DRY WEATHER

A few easy tricks for dealing with drought

DROUGHT-TOLERANT VEGETABLES AND HERBS

- Amaranth
- Broccoli
- Chards
- Chinese cabbage
- Eggplant
- Garlic chives
- German chamomile
- Lavender
- Malabar spinach
- Mustard greens
- Native strawberries
- Oregano
- Peas and beans—black-eyed peas, tepary beans, garbanzo beans, asparagus bean, snap and pole beans
- Peppers
- Rhubarb
- Rosemary
- Sage
- Thyme
- Tomatoes
- Winter savory

WITH MANY PARTS of the world suffering from drought, it is more important than ever to hack out your own solutions for smart, sustainable growing. It starts with plant selection. All herbs and vegetables need water and sunlight, but there are a number of herbs and vegetables that do remarkably well with little water.

To create a drought-tolerant herb and vegetable garden, you will need to plant in well-drained but moisture-retentive soil. Adding organic soil amendments to your ground and container plantings saves water and watering time because a garden with richer soil typically needs less water. Using techniques such as intensive planting will keep moisture at the root level for a longer period of time (see Hack 26: "Pack Your Plants in Tightly"). Have your soil professionally tested first to see what it might be lacking before making a final determination on soil amendments. Adding compost, worm castings, and other organic amendments to the soil followed by annual mulching will all help hold moisture and nutrients in the root area.

Water before 9 a.m. and after 7 p.m. to take advantage of reduced water evaporation rates. Use drip systems whenever possible; they are more water efficient than hose watering and sprinklers. Also, planting earlier in spring and later in fall means plants will be exposed to cooler weather and have less demanding water schedules. Planting taller plants such as eggplant and tomatoes next to leafy herbs and vegetables that tolerate shade well—such as chard and mustard greens—will help conduct heat better. Cooler gardens need less water.

DROUGHT-TOLERANT SOIL MIX

- 1 part organic potting soil
- 1 part organic rotted composted manure
- 1 part plain compost
- ¼ part worm castings

< Swiss chard 'Bright Lights' is a marvelous addition to a drought-tolerant vegetable container or bed; it has an astounding and beautiful color range.

59

BURY TOMATO PLANTS DEEP
Lower stems will turn into healthy roots

WHILE THERE ARE hundreds of varieties of tomatoes, there are two common types of tomato plants, each of which have unique growing forms: indeterminate and determinate. Choosing the best way to plant tomatoes does depend on which category the plant belongs in.

All tomatoes perform better when you plant them in a well-drained site with full sun (at least six hours of sun). Before planting, amend the soil with organic material, dig your hole, place organic fertilizer in the hole, then plant the tomato like any other plant. Stake or support the plant, then water at the base of the plant—not on the leaves—keeping the soil regularly moist throughout the season and mulching to prevent calcium deficiencies. Rotate crop locations annually. Increased production and root development can occur with additional feedings throughout the season using organic fertilizers such as rotted manure and fish emulsion.

Determinate tomatoes should be planted in a hole using the above-mentioned soil amendments. Do not plant it too

< Laying non-grafted indeterminate tomatoes on their sides in a trench at planting time can increase root growth along the stem, giving the plant a boost in growth and production.

DETERMINATE VERSUS INDETERMINATE VERSUS GRAFTED

- **Determinate** Most typically determinate varieties of tomatoes are considered "bush tomatoes" and reach a specific height and width, then stop growing taller. All of their fruit becomes ripe around the same time. While they still might need a supportive cage, these are excellent plants for small areas, patios, and containers.
- **Indeterminate** Varieties that are indeterminate will produce tomatoes for an extensive garden season, growing in vine form 5 to 10 feet and taller with continual flowering and fruit development. They often need extensive staking and pruning. Indeterminate tomatoes take up more space, but offer longevity in the garden with continual tomato production throughout the season.
- **Grafted** Grafting tomatoes is a creative way of strengthening an heirloom tomato. The root stock of an heirloom is grafted to a modern hybrid. Grafted tomatoes provide a 30 to 50 percent increase in tomato production and have resistance to pests and disease, so these plants have become extremely popular with modern gardeners.

∧ Indeterminate cherry tomatoes do particularly well when grown with the side-planting technique.

HOW TO PLANT AN INDETERMINATE TOMATO

1. Dig a wide trench approximately 3 inches shorter than the height of the plant. The trench should be 2 inches deeper than the root ball.
2. Amend the soil as recommended above.
3. Snip all the lower leaves and branches off the stem, only keeping the top 5 to 6 inches of tomato plant leaf.
4. Lay the tomato on its side in the trench with the top leaf portion sticking up out of the ground.
5. Bury the entire plant up to the leaves—leaving the leaves open to the air.
6. Water well and keep watered evenly.
7. Stake the plant well as it grows and fertilize organically throughout the season.

deep or the short, stocky plant will not be high enough above the ground to be supported. Grafted tomatoes have the same soil needs, but the graft line on the plant must be planted above the soil line, with no vining branches touching the ground or the plant will revert to its original form and not perform well.

Indeterminate tomatoes, however, can be planted in a unique way that will increase root production and organic nutrient absorption. This, in turn, will build a stronger root system and plant, enabling the plant to perform better over the tomato-growing season.

HACK GARDEN HERBS FOR EDIBLE FLOWERS

Flavorful herbs with colorful and delicious flowers

HERBS HAVE SOME of the most beautiful flowers in the garden world, and they are edible. This means you can harvest the flowers and use them for cooking, salads, or drinks any time in the growing season. Make an herb produce more flowers by following the tips below.

Herbs perform best when you plant them in a well-drained site with six to eight hours of full sun. When planting an herb that you want to flower, amend the soil with organic material, dig a hole, place organic flower fertilizer in the hole, then plant the herb. Water at the base of the plant—not on the leaves—keeping the soil regularly moist throughout the season. Mulch regularly to help keep weeds down.

Good soil drainage prevents fungal issues. Heavy manure content or highly rich soil can trigger more leaf growth. Additionally, over-fertilizing produces too much leaf and not enough flowers. Therefore, be sure to follow organic fertilizer package directions when amending the soil.

Herbal edible flowers look gorgeous floating in cocktails or topping salads or desserts. Some edible flowers are spicy, while others are mild—grow and experiment at will. Use just the petals or the whole flower to make a beautiful and artistic statement while entertaining.

10 FLOWERING EDIBLE HERBS AND THEIR FLOWER COLORS

• Anise hyssop	Purple
• Dill	Yellow
• Garlic chives	Purple and white
• Greek oregano	White
• Lavender	Lavender
• Pineapple sage	Red
• Purple basil	Purple
• Rosemary	White and lilac
• Thai basil	White and purple
• Spearmint	White and pink

∧ Chives make delightful edible raw treats on salads or in dressings, have beautiful short-lived cut flowers, and can be lovely pollinator plants.

61

REGROW FOOD FROM CUT KITCHEN SCRAPS

New life for lemongrass, lettuce, and more

FRESH ORGANIC VEGETABLES can be expensive unless you grow them from seed yourself. Another way to get new, cheap, organic vegetables is to save your cut vegetable scraps from the compost bin and regrow your own plants. It is important to select organic plants to regrow because organic foods have not been sprayed with growth-inhibiting chemicals. Plus, chemical-free vegetables are healthier for you.

HOW TO REGROW GINGER AND GARLIC

Place the ginger or garlic on its side in a container of soil. Water and fertilize regularly with organic fertilizer. Both plants take nearly a year to harvest.

HOW TO REGROW AN ONION

Plant the onion scrap root end down into the soil. Keep moist. Relocate to a larger planting area once greens begin to sprout.

HOW TO REGROW CELERY, BOK CHOY, CABBAGE, AND ROMAINE LETTUCE

These vegetables are easiest to regrow, especially when they have been harvested so that the bottom part of their.stems stay together and have a bit of root structure remaining. Once you have chopped off the celery stems or the leafy greens, set the remaining base of the vegetable in a bit of water, leaving the top open to the air. Refresh the water in the container several times per week. Once healthy tops start to grow on the plant, place the new plant base in organic soil, water regularly, and wait for it to grow. If needed, transfer it to the garden or a large container once it reaches a larger size. Cut the entire plant once it reaches mature size in 60 to 90 days or more.

∧ Leeks do particularly well when regrown because their root systems are often already developed when collected at the grocer.

HOW TO REGROW LEMONGRASS, LEEKS, FENNEL, AND SCALLIONS

Place the root ends in a vase of water, and change water daily. Once roots develop, pull the plant out and place it in organic soil and water regularly. Snip off greenery as needed.

HOW TO REGROW A PINEAPPLE

Cut the green leafy top off of the pineapple. Leaving the leafy part above the water, soak the bottom of the cut piece in a vase of water until roots develop. Once roots develop, place the plant in a container with lots of organic material mixed in the soil. Regrowth will take two to three years.

62
PLANT GROCERY STORE POTATOES
Organic super market spuds make stellar seed stock

JUST AS YOU can regrow food from cut organic kitchen scraps, you can also save a lot of money by getting your potato starts at the grocery store. It's important to select organic potatoes, as non-organic foods are often sprayed with chemicals designed to prevent sprouting.

Potatoes from the traditional grocery store come in several limited varieties, such as reds, russets, Yukons, and sweet potatoes or yams. Organic grocers are more likely to have more varieties to choose from, including white and red sweet potatoes; Japanese, jewel, and garnet yams; and small potatoes such as fingerlings and the Russian banana. Should you require more exotic or unique potato varieties, it is better to go the traditional route of purchasing through an organic grower or catalog.

< Varieties of potatoes are more likely to be unique at specialty stores and organic groceries.

> Once planted in the soil, the eyes of the potatoes will begin to grow as roots, reaching down below the surface of the soil.

< Get fresh potato starts from the organic section of the grocery store; cut each organic potato into two to three pieces. Each piece should have potato eyes.

HOW TO PLANT STORE-BOUGHT POTATOES

1. Bring the organic potatoes home and wash them.
2. Let dry thoroughly.
3. Cut each potato into two to three pieces, making sure that each piece has several "eyes." These eyes will be where the new growth sprouts.
4. Plant in the spring in a sunny location in well-draining soil in a potato planting bag or 12 inches apart in the ground. Amend soil as needed with organic matter before planting.
5. Harvest late in the summer immediately after the vines die, usually late in August.
6. Potatoes can be stored for a very long time; place them in a cool dark place after harvesting.

63

PLANT GLOBE BASIL TO WARD OFF RABBITS

Bunnies do not find the aroma divine

RABBITS ARE NOT fond of certain scents in the garden; old-fashioned marigold, agastache, artemesia, oregano, nepeta and mints, buddleia, Russian sage, salvia, and basil are just a few they find distasteful. They also do not typically like spiky or stiff plants such as achillea, agave, alocasia, asarum, asclepias, ferns, baptisia, carex, colocasia, echinacea, hellebores, heuchera, and pachysandra because they find them tough to chew or distasteful. Any animal, if it is starving, will not be deterred permanently by a heavily scented or spiked plant. However, building a border of spikes or scent to help wave the animal away is a smart hack for your garden.

Unfortunately most marigolds no longer have the extra-strong scent that used to be your grandmother's old-fashioned smelly marigold. Hybridization helped reduce the scent of the marigold to a milder level. But if you can find a plant that is equally strong smelling, you have a better chance of pushing the rabbits away from your garden, at least as their first choice.

Spicy globe basil and other spiky, small-leaved basils are remarkably rabbit resistant because they present an

< Planting globe basil around your garden can help deter rabbits, which are not fond of the smell.

HOW TO GROW
GLOBE BASIL

Globe basil prefers a sunny location that gets at least six hours of sun per day. Grow from seeds or transplants in well-drained soil that is richly amended with rotted manure or compost. Seed should be started two weeks after the last frost. Place seeds onto prepared soil, cover with ⅛ inch of soil, and keep moist until transplant. When watering basil, always water at the base of the plant to prevent fungal issues on leaves.

< Globe basil has a mounded habit, bold green leaves, a heavenly scent, and very tight-growing tiny leaves.

impenetrable wall of smell when planted as a tight fence around your garden. When faced with a smelly (to rabbits—not you) barrier of rounded basil, these pests err to the side of caution and go the other way. Again, this is not a 100-percent solution, but it definitely helps. An added bonus is the delicate white flowers that come out at the end of the season; these can be used in cooking, and they attract pollinators. The herb smells great to humans, and it is also incredibly tasty in salads, Mediterranean dishes, cocktails, and is wonderful when used for aromatherapy.

GARDEN WITH SHADE-TOLERANT EDIBLES
Shade is a great place to grow leafy herbs and vegetables

THINKING OUTSIDE THE BOX is easy when you have a little soil, a little water, and a whole lot of determination. Traditionalists believe that full sun is the most important ingredient to success for herbs and vegetables, yet not everyone gets six to eight (or more) hours of sun per day on their homes and balconies. Some get only partial sun and shade (four to six hours of sunlight per day), and others have full shade (less than four hours of direct sunlight per day).

When considering herbs and vegetables for lower light conditions, remember that shade equals no fruits and no roots. In other words, large fruiting plants such as tomatoes cannot produce abundantly in shade. Neither can root plants such as potatoes and beets. Growing root vegetables in shade means you will get far more leaf than root. It's the same with the fruiting plants; you'll get lots of greenery and very little fruit production. Having said that, perhaps that is what you want? Bull's blood beets are stunning plants with deep burgundy leaves that are delightful in a salad and present well in ornamental edible containers and beds. Growing for the leaf is as valid as growing for the roots because it still provides beauty and nutrition.

Vegetable and herb plants growing in shade have the same soil requirements as full sun plants; rich and well-drained organic matter is perfect. However, the watering needs of plants grown in the shade can be significantly different. Water at the base of the plants with a timed drip system before 9 a.m. or after 7 p.m. if possible to prevent fungal issues. Growing shade vegetables is easy and a fantastic solution for tight spaces such as balconies, patios, and fence lines.

^ These Malabar spinach wire towers at the Chicago Botanic Garden are surrounded by Swiss chard and other vegetables, growing successfully with six hours or less of sunlight per day.

< Bull's blood beets, curly parsley, and dinosaur kale make a delicious ornamental edible shade garden combination.

SOME SHADE-TOLERANT HERBS AND VEGETABLES

- Arugula
- Basil
- Beans
- Beet greens
- Celery
- Collards
- Corn mache
- Endive
- Herbs (chives, cilantro, lemon balm, mint, oregano, parsley, scallions, tarragon)
- Kale
- Lettuces
- Malabar spinach
- Mustard greens
- Pak choi
- Peas
- Radishes
- Rhubarb
- Spinach
- Swiss chard
- Turnip greens

GROW A GARDEN IN A PUBLIC RIGHT-OF-WAY

Turn a "hell strip" into a heavenly garden

ACROSS THE NATION, there is an epidemic of common grass growing in city right-of-way properties. Grass can look clean and attractive in public areas, but it requires a lot of maintenance. Commercial landscape equipment accounts for two-thirds of all gas-powered lawn and garden equipment. This means that cities and corporate and public spaces can have some of the biggest non-road toxic and carcinogenic emissions problems. Benzene, butadiene, and formaldehyde are among the top cancer-causing compounds emitted by the landscaping equipment. Carbon dioxide fumes and gasoline vapors also contribute to elevated risk of cancers in our communities.

With all that in mind, hacking a beautiful right-of-way garden for mixed ornamental edibles and perennial plantings makes a lot of sense: You are helping your community build a cleaner ecological environment, and building a garden that can improve property value and increase pollinator populations. In order to plant on right-of-way property, you will need to approach your city, your homeowner's association, or both with a formal plan. Apply for permission, pay any fees, and jump into gardening. If you do not ask permission up front, you may be faced with fines at a later date.

To create a mixed bed of vegetables, herbs, and perennials, start by enriching the soil. Have the soil tested to see if there are chemicals or other concerns for edible crops; with soil test results in hand, build a plan for amendments. Start by killing the grass by sheet mulching or by smothering (see Hack 80: "Hack Away Grass By Smothering It"), then amend the soil with organic and natural ingredients as

∧ This behind-the-fence garden is planted for the benefit of the community along a sidewalk. Cabbage is tucked beneath the park bench, cucumbers grow up the climbing frames, and herbs are strewn throughout the bed.

suggested by your testing. Common amendments include rotted manure, compost, and worm castings.

Planting drought-tolerant native flowers such as black-eyed Susans or echinacea next to vegetables and herbs is a brilliant idea for a hot, dry, right-of-way area or hell strip because the drought-tolerant plants work to shade the vegetables and herbs. Tucking the herbs and vegetables in between the sun lovers, beneath park benches, and next to your gates can help create a lovely garden that offers both food and health for the neighborhood.

UPCYCLE CORRUGATED PANELS
In raised beds, they will outlast most wood products

RECYCLED CORRUGATED PANELS (iron, zinc, or plastic) are strong, longer-lasting raised bed garden building materials than wood. Studies have been done in consideration of zinc leaching from soils next to galvanized structures. According to the International Zinc Association, it is a minimal effect that's well within the EPA guidelines. If you are concerned about exposure to metals or plastic, line your raised bed with a protective lining. Landscape fabric is not thick enough for this purpose, but EPDM rubber is a good choice. It is commonly used by drinking water companies to line drinking water storage tanks because it does not degrade or release material into the water over time. Do your research and find what works best for you and your family.

In these Chicago-area church garden photos, you see assembled corrugated panels with galvanized trim and metal rebar placed in the ground as extra support. Building your raised beds with heavy-duty cedar boards on the exterior of the panels will enable you to raise the bed higher.

∧ Planting a raised bed garden made from recycled or recyclable materials is an attractive solution for a home garden. *Photo credit: Andrea Duclos of www.ohdeardrea. blogspot.com.*

< Building a raised bed from long-lasting materials that are recycled or that can be recycled is a better environmental choice.

Andrea Duclos of www.ohdeardrea.blogspot.com has an amazing set-up in her garden using corrugated raised beds. Below are her specific directions for making one 12×3×1-foot raised bed.

HOW TO MAKE A CORRUGATED PANEL RAISED BED

1. Lay four of the 16-inch 2×4s on the ground spaced 2 feet apart.
2. Set one of the 12-foot metal pieces on top of the 16-inch stakes.
3. Make all of the stakes flush with one side of the metal. The stakes will extend 2 inches past the other side.
4. Screw directly through the sheet metal into the wood using three screws for each stake.
5. Do this one more time to make two 12-foot sides.
6. Clear bed site of weeds, grass, and other debris.
7. Dig footers for the stakes. There are eight stakes, so you will need eight holes that are each 2 to 3 inches deep.
8. Lay one of the long built sides in the footer holes with the metal facing in.
9. Fill in the holes with soil so the side stands on its own.
10. Do this again for the other side.
11. Once the long sides are in, screw the two 3-foot metal side pieces into place.
12. Now screw the top frame boards to their appropriate sides by laying them on top of the stakes. Use one screw for each stake (line beds with rubber if you are concerned about the soil contacting the metal).
13. Fill with soil, amend with compost and manure, plant a garden, and mulch.

∧ Planting a raised bed garden made from recycled or recyclable materials is an attractive solution for a home garden. *Photo credit: Andrea Duclos of www.ohdeardrea.blogspot.com.*

SUPPLIES NEEDED

- Two 12×1-foot corrugated metal roofing panels (side)
- Two 3×1-foot corrugated metal roofing panels (side)
- Eight 16-inch-long 2×4-inch rough cedar boards (stakes)
- Two 12-foot-long ¾×4-inch rough cedar boards with mitered 45-degree edges (top frame)
- Two 3-foot long ¾×4-inch rough cedar boards with mitered 45-degree edges (top frame)
- Twelve No. 8×1¼-inch coarse screws

- One pack 1½-inch drive straight hex sheet metal screws with washers
- Cordless drill (with hex and Phillips bits)
- Spade shovel (if cutting materials yourself)
- Circular saw (for cutting the metal and wood to size)
- Framing square
- Sharpie and a pencil

CONTAINER
hacks

HACKS IN THIS CHAPTER

USE COFFEE FILTERS TO STRAIN THE DRAIN
Basket filters are instant liners for pots

∧ Start with an empty container with drain holes.

WATERING PLANT CONTAINERS can leave soil, debris, and stains on the ground or table beneath your container because debris leaks out through the drain holes. To prevent this problem without restricting drainage, simply line the garden container with an unbleached coffee filter. It's one of the simplest container garden hacks ever.

Unbleached filters can be used in making compost: when you are done with your soil for the season, simply toss it and the coffee filter onto your compost pile.

∧ Place coffee filter liner at the bottom of the container. It will help block soil and debris from coming out the drain holes.

∧ Fill container with soil and plant up.

HIDE AN UGLY FENCE OR WALL
Give it a vertical-garden facelift

CREATING A BEAUTIFUL wall garden out of an ugly old brick or cement fence is a simple project with lovely results. Drought-tolerant and shallow-rooted plants such as hens and chicks, stonecrop, woolly thyme, English thyme, mint, creeping jenny, oregano, lamb's ears, and various cacti or succulents work best. Shallow root systems enable the plants to hang on well and stay healthy even with the limited growing area at the root.

Important to this growing technique are niches within the fence or wall that are just large enough for a small root system to attach so that the plant can hold on even with limited growing conditions. Pockets or cracks in stone masonry also work well, but keep in mind that placing a large-rooted plant in a cracked area can expand the crack and cause more damage, so using small-rooted plants that can handle drier conditions should be considered.

∧ Planting the niches in a cement or brick fence can make a surprisingly beautiful vertical display in the garden. *This photo was taken at the garden of Derk DeWit at the DeWit Tools Factory in the Netherlands.*

SUPPLIES NEEDED

- Drought-tolerant, shallow-rooted plants
- Cactus or succulent soil (you can make your own with 1 part potting soil, 1 part perlite or pumice, and 1 part coarse builder's sand)
- Organic fertilizer
- Gloves
- Spray hose with rain nozzle, water

HOW TO GROW PLANTS ON FENCES AND WALLS

1. Wash the wall down, scrubbing if necessary, to remove stains and chemicals.
2. Let the wall dry.
3. Mix up your cactus soil, add organic fertilizer according to package directions, and moisten the mix so that it is damp without being muddy.
4. Using gloved hands, take a handful of soil and pack it into cracks and niches within the stone, cement, or brick fence or wall.
5. Gently press the roots of the plants into the wall, being sure to press the roots as deeply as possible into the niches without breaking the plant stems.
6. Watch the wall carefully for the first few weeks to make sure the roots take hold and don't fall back out onto the ground—if a plant falls out, try relocating to a different part of the wall.
7. Water as you would a cactus or succulent using a rain-style nozzle with a gentle stream of water.

69

BUILD A GARDEN TOWER

Put your old planting containers to work

RECLAIMING OLD MATERIAL and finding fun ways to make it new again is an easy way to contribute to a sustainable community. All gardeners have a stack of old garden containers tucked away, which makes this garden hack a no-brainer for the garden addict. When plastic containers get old they become faded and warped from the sun, but they have not out-lived their usefulness. Here's how to bring them back to life to build a tower.

> Place a recycled planting tower along a fence or wall for an unexpected spot of color in your garden.

SUPPLIES NEEDED

- Six garden containers of various sizes, from large to small
- Non-toxic paint
- Organic soil
- Organic fertilizer
- Suggested plants for this garden hack include sweet potato vine, petunia, and euphorbia
- Tall stake

HOW TO BUILD A GARDEN TOWER

1. Your design's location can be on soil or a solid surface, but it needs to be very flat and level. Because of its height, this container tower could lean against a fence or wall, which will offer it additional protection from heavy winds.
2. Position the largest garden container on the bottom to function as the foundation.
3. Fill this container with organic planting soil. Do not overfill; leave 2 inches of room at the top of the container so that the medium garden container will fit inside the larger container.
4. Insert a tall, thin garden stake in the soil, then feed the next largest container onto the garden stake by threading the stake through its drainage hole.
5. Position this container to center it so that the tower does not begin to lean to one side or the other.
6. Repeat the process, feeding each container onto the stake using their drainage holes until all the containers are evenly filled and stacked. Leave 1½ inches of open space at the top of the container.
7. Plant the garden containers with your favorite plants for the growing conditions, add organic fertilizer as you plant. Keep in mind the size the plants will be at full growth in order to prevent overplanting.
8. Water well.

BUILD A GARDEN PYRAMID
Create a classic container arrangement

CONTAINER GARDENING CAN be remarkably sustainable: start by reusing old containers, using your own organic soil, and planting organic plants grown from seed. Of course, do not use pesticides or herbicides. Another idea: stack containers in a pyramid formation so it's possible to plant more plants in less square feet and share the watering. By watering the top container first, the water will slowly trickle down to the other layers and help to conserve water.

This hack is very easy. Be sure the bottom containers are heavy so that the foundation of your tower is secure.

SUPPLIES NEEDED
- Three large garden containers
- Four medium garden containers
- Organic soil
- Organic fertilizer
- Suggested plants for this garden hack include begonia, chocolate mint, coleus, kale, and torenia

∧ This pyramid garden container hack is a creative way to fill an empty spot in the organic garden beds.

HOW TO BUILD A PYRAMID
1. Your garden container design location should be very flat and level. Whether placed on bare soil or patio, the area needs to be even.
2. Position 3 large garden containers that are the exact same size so that their sides touch and the containers can help support each other.
3. Fill the large garden containers with organic planting soil. Do not overfill: leave 2 inches of room at the top of the container so that the medium garden containers fit inside the larger containers.
4. Place 1 medium container inside each of the larger containers, on top of the soil. Move them so that their sides are touching and supporting one another.
5. Fill the 3 medium containers with soil, leaving 1½ inches of open space at the top of the container.
6. Double check that the containers are level.
7. Fill the last medium container with soil, leaving 1½ inches of open space at the top of the container.
8. Place the last medium container on the top of the stack, forming the pyramid shape.
9. Plant the garden containers with your favorite plants that are appropriate for the growing conditions, being sure to add organic fertilizer as you plant. Keep in mind how large the plants will eventually be in order to prevent overplanting.
10. Water well.

HACK A STRAWBERRY GARDEN FROM AN OLD LIGHT FIXTURE

Multiple shades means more berry plants

RECYCLE AN OLD bathroom light fixture and transform it into an attractive strawberry container garden with only a few easy steps. Find an old light fixture that has glass or plastic shades large enough to fill with soil and a plant; you might have one in your home or you could go to a thrift store, salvage yard, or antique store. Craigslist and eBay are also good resource ideas for this hack.

Light fixture container gardens are a decorative solution for outdoor garden rooms as they look particularly spectacular displayed on a tabletop. One advantage of this style of planter is it helps keep the invasive roots of the strawberry contained for the season. Remove it from the table in the fall, place the container along a path or patio, and cover the container with mulch; it will over-winter with ease.

HOW TO HACK STRAWBERRIES

1. Find an old bathroom light fixture and take off all the wires attached to it.
2. Lay the light fixture flat. Using a no- or low-VOC paint, paint the fixture with a primer coat, then a top coat.
3. Rescue several old light fixture glass shades that will fit over the light socket.
4. Once the paint has dried, place the glass shades upside down on the sockets.
5. Fill with organic soil amended with organic fertilizer.
6. Plant with strawberry starts, water well, and mulch to hold in extra moisture.
7. Set on a table or directly in the garden.

< Growing strawberry starts in a recycled bathroom light fixture is an easy hack project that does not require drilling because the containers allow drainage out the base of the glass shade.

KEEP SLUGS OUT OF PLANTING CONTAINERS
Legs are an obstacle for creatures with none

SLUGS CAN GET into any container that sits on the ground. But it is possible to deter the slugs by raising the container up on legs (see photo). Lifting the container up off the ground increases air circulation below the container and may create a drier environment, so adjust your watering accordingly. Pig troughs and feeding bins are absolutely perfect for this hack.

In addition to raising the container, here are a few more tips for dealing with slugs in container gardens:

- **Make it dry** In order to discourage slugs, keep your container soil on the dry side.
- **Add diatomaceous earth (DE)** Made from a powder made from ground-up fossilized crustaceans called diatoms, DE is a natural product that cuts into a slug's body, causing it to die of dehydration. Apply DE in dry weather by sprinkling it around the base of plants. Reapply after water has been applied to the area.
- **Handpicking** Very early on an overcast or rainy morning, go out to your container gardens and handpick the slugs, then place them in a bucket of soapy water made from non-toxic soap. Next day, toss the water and slugs into the compost.
- **Salt** Go out in the middle of the night while the slugs are at their most active and sprinkle them with salt. This can work, but can also increase salt levels in your container gardens, so use salt sparingly or as a last resort.

∧ Hack a slug solution by raising your container gardens off the ground. This helps keep slugs away during the wet season.

WHAT'S THE MATTER WITH SLUGS?

Slugs are soft-bodied nocturnal mollusks that absolutely adore feeding on foliage and making holes in vegetable leaves. They prefer cool, dark, moist environments, and they are a plague to gardeners with thickly mulched gardens because they are particularly fond of organic mulches as a habitat. Slugs have the disadvantage of not being able to move well unless the feeding areas and soil in their community is moist. They love the rainy season and reproduce exponentially at that time. They leave a sticky slimy trail behind them, particularly in drier areas. In a healthy eco-environmental garden, they can be controlled by natural slug predators such as frogs, toads, snakes, turtles, and ducks.

73

TREE STUMP CONTAINER GARDEN
Hollow one out and have a planter for years

WHAT DO YOU do with an old tree stump? Hack it, of course. You can create a beautiful and sustainable garden container from a stump. If you don't have an old stump, a great substitute would be a log that has been cut up, but make sure it rests evenly on the ground so you have a sturdy garden container.

The primary issue is creating a hole in the stump or log that will hold soil and plants. Rotted stumps are perfect as you can clear the rotted wood out using a hand mattock with no problem whatsoever. Healthier stumps might require a pickaxe or chainsaw to help remove the middle.

Before you start your project, determine what you want to plant in the stump. If your stump or log is in full, hot sun, you might want to plant succulents with a cactus soil mix. If it is in mostly shade, you might want to plant ferns with a soil mix heavy in humus. Your choice is dependent upon the conditions.

HOW TO CREATE A TREE STUMP CONTAINER
1. Start the container hole by hitting the middle of the stump with the pointy end of the mattock. See how it goes: If the middle comes out easily, continue. If you find it is more challenging, perhaps consider using a chainsaw to carve out the stump.
2. Carve out the center to create a hole that is 6 to 8 inches deep, and keep the side walls 2 to 3 inches thick.
3. Once the hole is chipped out, use the drill to make drain holes. Good drainage is important for container plants to prevent root rot. Drill four drainage holes out the bottom sides of the stump; angle out and down.
4. Fill the container with your favorite organic soil mix. Plant.

SUPPLIES NEEDED
- Mattock or pickaxe
- Chainsaw (optional)
- Drill with ½-inch bit
- Organic soil
- Plants

∧ In a shady woodland setting, ferns can be the perfect stump plant, requiring little attention. Tree stumps work well with succulents, ornamental edibles, and annual plants.

PUT BIG CONTAINERS ON A DIRT DIET
Some light fill keeps the weight down

MOVING CONTAINER GARDENS is hard on your back. But you may want to move certain garden containers from a full sun position in April to a part-shade, cooler position in late August to extend your growing season.

There is a simple garden hack to solve the problem of a heavy potted planter: Lighten the load. Fill the bottom of your containers with lightweight, food-safe recyclables. Do not use Styrofoam or other materials that put off toxic by-products or have toxic fumes, particularly when planting with herbs and vegetables.

HOW TO MAKE POTS LIGHTER
1. Obtain an empty potting container.
2. Fill the container bottom with lightweight, crushed recyclables like empty milk jugs and used plastic water bottles.
3. Cover with 8 to 12 inches of organic soil mix appropriate to the plants you will be growing.
4. Plant your plants.

< Start with a large garden container. Fill the bottom half of the container with lightweight, food-safe recyclables so that the container is lighter and easier to lift and move.

< Place the preferred soil mix on top of the recyclables, arranging plants carefully and planting.

75

UPCYCLE OLD FURNISHINGS

Outdoor furniture holds up the best

∨ Reusing an old chair or loveseat as a flowerpot is a creative way to display a container garden and makes a lovely addition to a patio or path.

FURNITURE OF ALL sorts is regularly thrown into landfills. In the United States alone, it is reported that furniture constitutes more than 9.8 million tons of the household waste in landfills, and that amount is growing. Reusing furniture in creative ways helps keep it out of the landfills longer, thereby creating a smart solution for the environment. Outdoor furniture—and wicker in particular—can be creative garden containers.

SUPPLIES NEEDED

- Something to transform into a flowerpot (an old chair works fine)
- Paint (preferably VOC-free), paintbrush, and tarp
- Something to prevent the soil from leaking out the bottom of the bin; old plastic storage bin lids or wood works fine
- Wire mesh, wire, and wire cutters
- Organic soil appropriate for growing your plant varieties
- Organic fertilizer
- Moss (if sphagnum moss is an environmental concern, try pit moss or another substitute)
- Plants

∧ Lay out all your supplies, protecting the ground against any paint overspray.

HOW TO UPCYCLE A WICKER CHAIR

1. Build the container area, making sure there is plenty of room for soil and plant roots—lay out a tarp, turn the chair over, lay old storage bin lids (or wood) down on the bottom, then cover with wire meshing by connecting with wire and wire cutters.
2. Prime paint first, if possible, then paint the top coat over the primer; this is optional as it is more environmentally sensitive to go without paint at all.
3. Place moss or moss substitute around the edges of the container area to prevent the soil from leaking out, soaking the moss first to expand it (substitute coconut coir, shredded leaves, or old greenery as a filler if you prefer).
4. Fill the container with potting soil mixed with organic fertilizer according to package directions.
5. Plant your favorite plants and water well.

∧ Be sure to cover the bottom of the container with wire mesh and something to hold the soil, such as wood or plastic.

∧ Paint the chair, wire and all, once you have it assembled the unit. This is optional, as going all-natural without the paint is certainly a smarter environmental choice.

∧ Soak moss or moss substitute and push gently around the edges of the chair to help prevent soil from leaking.

76

GROW A LIVING WALL

Create vertical gardens with purpose

∧ Planting a living wall next to a patio or seating area helps provide a bit of beauty and it helps build a remarkable outdoor room.

PLANTING 35 TO 40 plants in less than 2 square feet is easily accomplished with a living wall garden. Growing a living wall is a remarkably easy way to hack a small space garden because it enables you to plant more plants on a fence, balcony, or patio, plus there's no weeding and you can conserve water. Whether you make your own living wall or purchase it, consider keeping the garden organic and healthy by installing your garden in a food-safe planting system. One way to hack a living wall is to purchase four or five wire window boxes, each lined with a coco liner. Hang them on a wall, fence, or gate, one on top of the other, leaving 6 inches of air space between each box.

STANDARD LIVING WALL SOIL MIX FORMULA
- 1 part organic potting soil with worm castings
- 1 part organic rotted, composted manure
- 1 part coarse builder's sand

CACTUS AND SUCCULENT LIVING WALL
SOIL MIX FORMULA
- 1 part organic potting soil with worm castings
- 1 part perlite or pumice
- 1 part coarse builder's sand

EXTREMELY WATER-RETENTIVE LIVING
WALL SOIL MIX FORMULA FOR DROUGHT
CONDITIONS (NEEDS STRONG DRAINAGE)
- 1 part organic potting soil with worm castings
- 1 part organic rotted, composted manure
- 1 part plain compost

Because living walls are raised up off the ground, they get more air circulation. Dependent upon your weather, this could mean that the living wall dries out quickly. With this in mind, the planting mix you use is key to the success of the living wall. For standard plantings, a heavier soil mix made for a living wall is important. For succulent gardening, a soil mix that drains well is critical. See the list of suggested soil formulas at left.

Planting a living wall is easy: hang a living wall window box series or system, select your soil based on the needs of the preferred plants, plant your garden, and water. It's an easy hack that enables you to grow a lot more plants in a ridiculously small space.

HACKING METAL FOR THE GARDEN
Wheel wells can work wonders

HUMANS THROW AWAY millions of tons of metals annually, stressing landfills across the world. Deposits of metals in landfills are predicted to be 40 to 50 times richer than mined ores from the ground. Reusing metals before they reach the landfills, particularly as garden hacks, is a smart way to help the environment.

Metal is perfect for all types of creative uses in the garden such as gates, walls, fences, sculptures, and container gardening. Pam Penick, author of *The Water Saving Garden: How to Grow a Gorgeous Garden with a Lot Less Water*, has an amazingly creative example of a recycled metal container hack. In the photo on this page, you see her front entry garden filled with steel pipe remnants and tractor rims she found on Craigslist for a song. She filled the iron pieces with a soil mix and plants, and the containers become garden art as much as functional growing basins.

Finding metal to use for your garden sculpture and containers is easy because there are many sources for reclaiming and reusing metals. Search online on Craigslist and eBay, in automotive repair shops, industrial welding shops, metal and discount steel stores, thrift stores, antique stores, salvage shops, and junkyards.

Using metal as functional art in the garden is an unexpected and sustainable garden hack that will have all your garden friends talking.

^ Using old metal containers is a tremendous way to hack a garden container, and it's a sustainable way to reduce, recycle, and reuse. *Photo taken at the garden of Pam Penick from Digging at www.penick.net.*

HACK YOUR HARDINESS ZONE

Burying pots provides insulation and allows for easy overwintering indoors

GARDEN CONDITIONS VARY based on seasonal weather changes. In order to track the changes, many countries follow a map guide. In the United States, for example, there is a USDA Plant Hardiness Zone Map, which helps gardeners and farmers have a better understanding of their area's planting seasons. Labels on seed and plant packages list zone aptitude so you know if a plant is fit for the weather where you want to plant it.

Sometimes, though, gardeners want to place a plant in the garden that is outside of their weather zone. Planting a very tropical Zone 10 plant in a chilly Zone 5 area means that the tropical plant will die when the cold sets in and not overwinter. Hacking that situation is simple: plant your out-of-zone plant in a container, dig a hole in the ground, and plant the freshly potted plant in the ground. Then, just before the cold season sets in, pull the potted plant out and store it for the winter in a greenhouse or indoors near a sunny window.

< In this photo, you can see an agave, which is not winter tolerant, that has been placed in a ground in its container below soil level. The plant looks like it belongs in the space year round, but it is pulled out—pot and all—and overwintered in a greenhouse each winter. *Photo credit: Kylee Baumle from www.ourlittleacre.com in her beautiful northwestern Ohio garden.*

< Vertical planters that hang on your outdoor walls are another option for making your cold-averse plants portable.

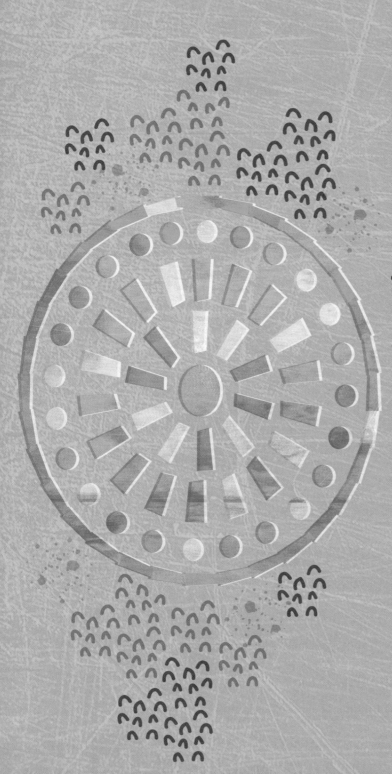

LANDSCAPE
hacks

HACKS IN THIS CHAPTER

79

CARDBOARD SHEET MULCH LINING
Lay down a layer of cardboard as a base for planting beds

CARDBOARD IS EASILY found at fast food restaurants, supermarkets, and from boxes sent by nearly any online store. We are surrounded by corrugated cardboard that's used for transport packaging, food packaging, and decorative boxing. Sadly, the current recycling rate for paper and board packing waste is only 49 percent, according to a Green Industries study on food packaging wastes and environmental impacts. That means that 51 percent of cardboard products are not recycled.

What happens to that wasted cardboard? Typically, it is thrown into landfills or burned, which are not environmentally sustainable practices. Utilizing cardboard as a mulch is a sustainable and creative way to hack your cardboard: It keeps the cardboard out of the landfill while functioning as a mulch and weed block for your garden. Most importantly, it can be an important component of sheet mulching—also known as "lasagna gardening"—which is an easy way to build a no-dig garden that does not require tilling. Using this technique, which was originally popularized in the late 1990s by Patricia Lanza's creative book, *Lasagna Gardening*, can help you build a rich soil within a few short seasons.

HOW TO SHEET MULCH

1. In the late fall, mow or cut your vegetation to the ground.
2. Cover your garden area with a thick layer of flattened cardboard boxes.
3. Spread a 2-inch layer of wood chips on top of the cardboard.
4. Cover the garden area with a thick layer of newspaper, then water the area well.
5. Add a 2-inch layer of dried grass clippings mixed with rotting food compost.
6. Add a thick layer of chopped fall leaves.
7. Cover the garden area with another thick layer of newspaper, then water the area well.
8. Add a 2-inch layer of mixed fresh vegetable compostables mixed with other compost matter such as coffee grounds and sand.
9. Add a 2-inch layer of rotted manure.
10. Top off the layers with a heavy layer of compost.
11. Wait patiently until spring, then dig planting holes directly through the layers and plant the garden.
12. Mulch around the plants to help keep weeds down and moisture at the roots of the plants.
13. Once a sheet mulch garden is established, place cardboard around the plants before covering with compost and wood chips.

ˇ Placing cardboard as the first layer of your sheet-mulched garden helps kill the grass and weeds beneath. Once a sheet mulch garden is established, place cardboard around the plants before covering with compost and wood chips.

HACK AWAY UNWANTED GRASS BY SMOTHERING IT
Create new beds without using chemicals

GETTING RID OF grass and weeds can be an immense problem in gardens. In order to kill large sections of grass without spraying chemicals, there are a number of easy—and super cheap—hacks to choose from.

CARPET OR BURLAP

One of the most effective techniques for smothering grass is to lay carpet over the grass for the winter season. Carpet allows water to seep through but not sunlight. The moisture and lack of sun eventually cause the grass and weeds beneath it to die. The problem with carpet is that some have a high chemical content. If you can, it is healthier if you choose a carpet made from natural fibers like abaca, raffia, seagrass, wool, hemp, cotton, and other natural blends with a natural rubber backing. Burlap also works well, but it will need to be doubled in order to block out the light properly.

∧ Killing the grass by smothering it is possible if the grassy or weedy area is covered for several months. There are several techniques: you can use carpet, burlap, newspaper, cardboard, or plastic sheeting. *Photo credit: Charles Dowding of www.charlesdowding.co.uk.*

NEWSPAPER OR CARDBOARD

Cover the grass you want killed with a very thick layer of newspapers in the fall. Twelve to fifteen newspaper layers thick should work. Water the top of the newspapers and cover all the edges with something heavy so that once the papers dry out, they will not blow away. Old garden containers or rocks work well for weighting the papers down. Another idea is to cover the newspaper with mulch or wood chips until you choose to uncover it in the spring. Leave the papers on top of the grass all winter for best success. You can do this same process with thick cardboard.

SOLARIZATION

Cover the grass with a double layer of heavy plastic sheeting in a full sun area during a hot spring or summer. Black plastic heats up the most, but clear or white plastic also works. Plastic traps the heat and kills both grass and seeds. Stake the plastic down on the sides so it does not blow away in the wind. Keep the plastic on the ground for four to six months. There are some concerns that solarization might affect beneficial microorganisms in the soil. If this is a concern for you, the newspaper method might be the best option.

81

MAKE A CREATIVE LANDSCAPE
BORDER WITH STICKS

Protect plants and create some visual relief

DEFINING YOUR GARDEN beds with borders helps make them look more decorative; it outlines planted areas and can contain certain plants. Garden hack your flowerbeds or herb gardens with a border made from sticks—it's a smart and sustainable way to reuse prunings from your shrubs and trees, much better than throwing them into a landfill or burning them. Reusing natural items in the garden helps create a sustainable solution for your clippings.

Freshly pruned green stems and sticks work best as edging because they are flexible and less brittle. Once formed into a shape, the lopped limbs shrink a bit as they dry and tighten themselves into position. There are many ways to reuse green limbs and saplings for border and fencing purposes: Braiding, wattle weaving, and simple loop are just a few. Simple loop is the easiest of these techniques and is made by bending green, pliable branches into arches and placing them along your borders and paths. Follow the directions below.

SUPPLIES
NEEDED
- Loppers
- String
- Gloves (optional)

∧ This stick border was created to protect an early spring garden from foot traffic. Hacking a stick border is an easy and natural way to protect and decorate your paths and garden beds.

HOW TO MAKE A STICK BORDER

1. Prune stems or sticks off of shrubs or trees with loppers.
2. Lay out stems and stick trimmings side by side.
3. Tie with string to help hold the lengths together.
4. Trim to the desired length; be sure to make all the sticks the same length. Untie the bundle.
5. Take one stick and push one end into the ground 1 to 2 inches.
6. Carefully arch the stick and press the other end of the stick tip into the ground 1 to 2 inches.
7. Repeat this process, slightly overlapping the sticks so that a scalloped, arching fence shape begins to form.
8. Creating this stick border garden hack is a natural way to build a decorative border for garden beds, walkways, or individual plants.

< Wattle-style weaving with your leftover branches and sticks works well as a temporary border solution.

HACK A PLANTING GUIDE WITH FLOUR
An all-natural hack using a common kitchen find

USING INTENSIVE PLANTING techniques (see Hack 26: "Pack Your Plants in Tightly") it is possible to plant closely together in containers and in the ground and still maintain consistent moisture at the root level. It also enables the planting of creative, non-traditional designs, whether they are purely artistic or edible.

Traditional garden design advice suggests marking off the planting area with spray paint on the ground. However, there is no need to add paint chemicals to your garden beds when you can use an all-natural product to delineate the space. While laying out garden hoses works well to delineate gentle curves, they are not as effective for tight designs and spaces. Instead, use unbleached flour. Garden designs are easily marked and erased and remarked again until you find just the right shape for your in-ground garden art.

HOW TO LAY OUT A PLANTING AREA WITH FLOUR

1. Amend the garden soil and prepare beds as needed.
2. Sprinkle flour on the ground to delineate your design. Correct mistakes until you are positive you have the right shape. Some trial-and-error is usually necessary.
3. Place plants inside the designs to make sure everything lines up.
4. Plant your garden and wait for the results.

∧ Instead of using spray paint to lay out garden designs, consider a healthier environmental choice and use flour instead.

∧ Once the design has been delineated with flour, plant your garden up and await the fantastic results.

HACK A GARDEN BORDER
WITH JUST ABOUT ANYTHING
Found objects are fun and free to use

For a super easy, no-dig garden border, consider outlining your garden beds with a repetitive pattern made from collected item. First, make sure there is a crisp delineation between your border and what surrounds it. Use an edger or shovel to cut a crisp line between the garden bed and its edge. Then set the border along the line that you cut. Using the same item over and over helps as it establishes a pattern. In this hack, there is no digging or permanent placement, so you can choose to change out the design from year to year or keep it in place permanently.

There are many items you can use to create a repetitive pattern. They can serve as a visual aid, telling visitors where the border to the garden is, and also as a way to hold plants in the bed. Salvage yards, construction sites, and websites such as freecycle.org or Craigslist often have interesting and inspired items at low to no cost. Do not put recycled or reused items that have been exposed to chemicals or toxins in your garden. Here are a few examples of items you might consider.

- Bamboo
- Bowling balls
- Glass insulators
- Logs
- Terra cotta flower pots
- Large clam shells
- River rocks
- Old bricks
- Hubcaps
- Slag glass

- Roofing tiles
- Cement blocks
- Flour grinding stones
- Metal pipes
- Clay pipes
- Old fence posts
- Railroad sleepers
- Truck, tractor, and auto parts
- Stacked stone

∧ Antique glass insulators are a perfect edging for a garden border as they are easy to install and can be found in multiple colors that can enhance your garden design.

∧ Glass insulators border this garden bed and patio area, delineating the flagstone from the mulched soil edge.

< River rock or stone is beautiful and can often be found at construction sites and in farm fields at no cost, but be sure to ask permission before searching for stone in an area that is not your property.

HACK YOUR OWN GROUNDCOVER PATIO

Growing plants beneath your feet

THE EXPENSE OF building or rebuilding a patio can be quite high. If you'd like to add a patio or expand upon an existing construction, hack the project. There are plenty of free or very inexpensive materials that you can combine with groundcover to create a functional and natural outdoor living area. Pavers, patio blocks, steppingstones, or bricks are cheap and sometimes free, and they blend well with low-growing plants in a patio area. This can be non-permanent dependent upon your needs. Having plants beneath your feet while entertaining is such a green delight. Best yet, you can plant drought-tolerant groundcover plants such as hen and chicks, sedum, and thyme in order to save yourself money and time.

In the photos, you can see how concrete pavers were used (approximately 57 pounds each). Square patio blocks and pavers typically range from 12 inches to 24 inches in length and width. Measure the area you would like to fill with a groundcover patio, then leave 3 inches to 4 inches between pavers in order to allow for plants to reside. Avoid gaps any wider than that because it will encourage more weeds to fill in that space.

SUPPLIES NEEDED
- Concrete pavers, bricks, stepping stones, or tiles
- Drought-tolerant soil mix
- Organic fertilizer
- Sand for leveling
- Shovel
- Rake
- Level
- Drought-tolerant groundcover plants

HOW TO MAKE A GROUNDCOVER PATIO
1. Remove all grass or plants from the building area.
2. Amend soil for drought conditions (see Hack 4: "Hack Your Way Through a Dry Spell"), leveling with more soil, and raking the area flat.
3. Mark the area for block placement based on your measurements.
4. Place a 2-inch layer of sand over the area and level again carefully.
5. Place pavers in position, carefully maneuvering into your chosen pattern.
6. Mix the remaining drought-tolerant soil with organic fertilizer and fill the areas between bricks with the fertilized soil.
7. Plant the plants, then water well and wait for your plants to grow in.

> Geometric designs work best for groundcover-filled patios so that the straight lines enable the plants to spread and connect. Here is the design before it is planted.

> This expanded patio filled with groundcovers and color has been transformed into an outdoor garden room, perfect for outdoor entertaining.

WINE BOTTLE PATHWAY EDGING

Introduce some light and color into your garden

CLOSE TO A BILLION wine bottles are produced each year; they can be found for free at most any restaurant or in your very own recycling bin. Throwing glass in the garbage is a huge waste of our resources. Wine bottles specifically can be useful in the garden due to their thickness and strength. According to the US Environmental Protection Agency, only 34.5 percent of wine and liquor bottles are recycled annually. Do your part to help the environment by hacking your garden path with an attractive and fun wine bottle border.

HOW TO MAKE A WINE BOTTLE PATHWAY

1. Lay out the wine bottles along your path to make sure you have enough to cover the proposed area.
2. Dig a 3- to 6-inch-deep trench on the outside edges of the path.
3. Place a 2-inch layer of sand in the trench where the wine bottles are going to go.
4. Turn the wine bottles upside down and carefully place them side-by-side on the firmer side of the trench using the sand as a stabilizer to prevent the wine bottles from tipping.
5. Backfill with soil along the loose soil side of the wine bottles.
6. Push soil in place to hold the bottles in position.

SUPPLIES NEEDED
- Wine bottles (with or without wine labels)
- Sand
- Shovels

∧ Wine bottles are flipped upside down, angled, and buried on the edge of the path, creating a non-permanent border that nevertheless can last for years in the garden.

< Dig a trench and lay out the bottles in advance to make sure you have enough to cover the allotted space.

< Sand helps stabilize the wine bottles and also makes it easy to pull out and replace bottles as needed.

MAKE PRACTICAL LANDSCAPE SOLUTIONS
WITH RECLAIMED MATERIALS
Create a lovely patio area in an unplantable garden zone

WHAT HAPPENS WHEN your property is filled with tree roots or rocky areas that that would make adding structures difficult? Hacking a green and healthy solution from your challenging situation is easy: simply float a patio or a fun, ground-level art accent right on top of the obstructions. Using reclaimed sand, bricks, and stones helps make the project greener by keeping those materials out of the landfill.

ᵛ Building a recycled temporary or floating patio can be a lovely solution in a garden filled with roots or difficult soil.

SUPPLIES NEEDED	HOW TO CREATE A LANDSCAPE ACCENT
• Shovel • Thick landscaping fabric • Sand or paving base • Flat items including bricks, pavers, steppingstones, broken cement, rocks, log cuts, flagstone, non-hazardous construction materials, metal • Pea gravel, lime screenings, or granite	1. Mark off your building area shape and design on the ground. The area should be flat and relatively level. 2. Do your best to dig a 6- to 8-inch trench around the outside of your project area. This will allow standing water to drain off the area. This does not have to be perfect and can just involve several drain holes, but it allows for water to run off. 3. Cover the project area with a permeable cloth cover of some kind that will allow water to drain but will prevent worms from coming through and mixing the rock base. Landscape fabric or weed barrier is the logical choice for most installations. 4. Arrange reclaimed material of all types in an attractive pattern on top of the fabric. 5. Fill between the arranged material with a base of sand and rough gravel to help steady the reclaimed materials. Hardware and big box stores often have discounted broken bags. 6. Pour pea gravel over the top. For a firmer surface that can be used as a patio, use lime screenings or crushed granite that can be tamped down.

∧ Mark the perimeter of a flat area for your patio, dig drainage holes, and cover with a permeable cloth cover such as landscape fabric.

∧ Using flat, recycled materials from construction sites such as bricks and broken cement, create a pattern on the ground.

∧ Adjust and readjust the pattern as necessary until the design is to your liking.

> Cover the materials with a layer of sand and rough gravel. Top with pea gravel, lime screenings, or granite.

FREE PASS-ALONG PLANTS
Sharing plants and seeds is smart in many ways

HACKING FREE PLANTS for your garden is easy to do just by sharing and exchanging with neighbors, friends, and family. Pass-along plants are plants that have been owned by someone else, divided, and then given away at splitting or dividing time in a generous act of garden sharing. Vegetative plants can be expensive when purchased in bulk, so pass-along plants are a great way to save money and to help others with their gardens.

Most perennials need to be divided anyway, in order to continue to perform prolifically. They typically can be divided any time during the growing season; early spring works well, as does the fall on a cloudy day. Transplanting before a cooler season when the plants go dormant means there will be fewer water worries.

There are two ways to divide a plant. You can either dig up the entire plant, cut it into pieces with a shovel or spade, amend the soil in the garden bed, and replant the divisions, or you can use a shovel to cut up the plant while it is still in the ground. Simply slice through the middle of the plant. Then amend the soil in the next planting location and replant the divisions.

Watering the area before and after division helps loosen the plant and prevent root shock. Keep in mind that some plants do not like to be divided consistently. Additionally, some plants can become invasive in a new neighborhood, so giving them is not a gift but a scourge. Definitely research the garden plants you want to pass along before sharing with others.

∧ When your garden becomes jam-packed with perennials, it is time to divide and conquer. Pass these divided plants along to your family, friends, and community, and reap the rewards of saving money and sharing garden love.

> Asking friends and neighbors to help with the digging and dividing keeps the work to a minimum. Here gardeners help split perennials for a native prairie planting area in their community.

MULCH WITH SEASHELLS TO ADD CALCIUM
Choose a semi-permanent material that is slow to decompose

MULCHING YOUR GARDEN is generally thought of as the single-most important thing you can do to help maintain your garden beds. Regular mulching helps hold moisture in the soil, keeps root temperature even, and also controls weeds by either blocking or smothering out the weed seeds. By using natural mulch, you are also contributing to a stronger soil structure in the landscape. As the mulch breaks down, it is integrated into the soil, thereby creating a system that helps better support your plants. There are many types of natural mulch with strong organic matter percentages: Leaf mold, cocoa shell mulch, shredded bark, pine needles, straw, wood chips, and grass clippings, for instance. Even compost can be used as an effective mulch if a heavy layer is applied as a topdressing over the soil. Do not use horticultural fabric under mulch: weeds continue to form on top of the fabric and it does not allow nutrients to enter the root zone. Simply place the mulch directly on to the soil.

There are times, however, when it is appropriate to choose a mulch that does not break down as quickly. Decorative mulches with a long shelf life include lava rock, shale, river stone, small pebbles, lime and granite screenings, glass, and seashells. Utilizing seashells as mulch is an excellent garden hack (especially in areas where shells are used for road beds and are practically free) for adding calcium and phosphates to the soil as well as for deterring snails and other insects that do not like the sharp shell edges.

∧ Mulching with seashells adds calcium to garden beds and provides a heavier, more permanent solution for garden areas that need an ornamental or decorative mulch.

Much like pebbles, seashells help hold the soil in around a planting bed and keep the soil cool and moist. Although many companies are now dyeing seashells, it is better to choose an all-natural, undyed lot. Maintenance for this type of mulch is simple: Regularly blow debris off with a leaf blower. Seashells are not a solution for wet or consistently damp areas as the seashells will become overgrown with moss. Sunny sites are best. Eventually the seashells will start to decompose, but it takes years and years for this to happen, making them a decorative and creative mulch solution with longevity.

OUTDOOR living HACKS

HACKS IN THIS CHAPTER

89

A NO-DRILL, NO-SAW, NO-SCREW PARK BENCH
It's reclaimable, sturdy, and temporary

SUSTAINABILITY IS ABOUT supporting the environment by not depleting natural resources. Across the world, we see corporations that, as massive consumers, develop sustainability standards for their products. While this corporate sustainability movement is making an impact, it is not enough; all end-consumers should be thinking about sustainability and how we as individuals can affect the environment.

With this in mind, it is not simply one thing that makes a difference from a sustainability perspective, but the combined efforts of millions of people reducing, reusing, and recycling around the globe that create a positive environmental reaction. Why not find a way to use less in your gardening practices and help the planet more? There are some obvious ways to conserve in the garden: compost, save water, save seed, and do not use herbicides or pesticides. Another thought is to reuse old items in our outdoor garden rooms and use fewer resources in our building and design projects.

> Using a hacked sustainable bench as an accessory to an already sustainably designed garden can make a difference for the environment.

> Here we see a used wine bottle path, recycled raised beds, and a reclaimed arbor in a fashionably color-blocked garden area.

Outdoor living presents one of the more daunting sustainable challenges. In creating an outdoor living space, we use lots of tools and items to build; we gardeners sometimes need tools such as screws, hammers, levels, and saws to create seating and hardscaping in the garden.

One great garden hack idea is to create a no-drill, no-saw, no-screw park bench for your garden. This can be either a permanent or a temporary seating solution for your favorite little garden niche.

SUPPLIES NEEDED	HOW TO BUILD A PARK BENCH
• Twelve concrete blocks	1. Paint the concrete blocks the color of your choice. Let dry.
• Four cedar 4×4s	2. Make two side support towers of six blocks each and place on a level surface.
• Two cans one-coat paint	3. Thread the 4×4s through the top concrete blocks.
• Cushions for the finished project	4. Place cushions on top.

HANG A RECYCLED CHANDELIER IN YOUR GARDEN
Create beauty with a formal touch

REUSING AND UPCYCLING hits an all-new, beautiful hack-ability level when you start bringing crystal and elegance to the garden with chandeliers. While it is possible to hang working chandeliers outdoors, this particular hack works best for non-working chandeliers that need a new lease on life. If you're going to use chandeliers and keep the original hardware, electrical, and light bulbs, you will need to consult a professional electrician on the viability of making it work safely.

WHERE TO FIND OLD OR USED CHANDELIERS

- Antique shops
- Salvage yards
- eBay
- Freecycle.org
- Craigslist
- Thrift shops
- Habitat for Humanity ReStore
- Flea Markets
- Amazon.com

< Adding a recycled chandelier to an outdoor garden room can truly add some eye-appeal to the garden.

SUPPLIES NEEDED

- Soft cloth and a brush for cleaning
- Primer spray paint
- Spray paint
- Spray sealer
- Painter's tape
- Wire and a wire cutter (optional)

HOW TO BUILD A GARDEN CHANDELIER

1. Bring your old chandelier home and disassemble it
2. Carefully remove all crystal, hooks, or glass, placing the pieces in order on a flat surface so that you can reassemble it again after cleaning.
3. Cut off all wires and hardware you do not want to keep.
4. Completely clean all the parts with a brush and cloth.
5. Tape any parts you do not want painted.
6. Hang outdoors in a well-ventilated area for easy spray painting.
7. Apply two light coats of primer; let dry between coats.
8. Apply top coat of paint; let dry.
9. Apply sealer; let dry overnight.
10. Reattach any crystal or glass. Should any hooks break, simply reattach pieces using wire and a wire cutter.
11. Hang in the garden.

< Removing all the electrical fittings and wires, painting the chandelier, then reassembling the crystal on the chandelier keeps it out of the landfill and offers an interesting item for your patio.

HIDE THAT UGLY SHED

Retrofit a room divider as a visual screen

∧ Have an ugly shed at the end of your walkway or in your back garden? Get creative and put up an outdoor room divider to hide the view.

SHEDS DON'T HAVE to be viewed as a necessary evil in the garden; sometimes they are beautiful in their own right, but other times they need some help from you. Consider using a traditional room divider as a view block. Or you can find material to drill or tie together to create a screen: metal gates, salvage yard doors, tall window shutters, or arbor pieces all work well. In this case, four metal corners from a broken patio gazebo did the trick.

In order to build a screen, the gates, doors, shutters, or metal needs to be tall enough to cover the shed in question. Five-panel screens work the best because the paneling can be attached in such a way that it will not easily fall over in the garden. Straight panels with no bends must be attached to metal rods and inserted in the ground.

SUPPLIES NEEDED

- Screen material (tall gates, doors, shutters, or metal panels)
- Zip ties
- Screws and drill (optional—depends on if you need a steadier unit)
- Plastic tablecloths
- Wire and wire cutters

> Find metal gates, salvage yard doors, tall window shutters, or arbor pieces and assemble the pieces into a screen.

HOW TO CREATE A VISUAL SCREEN

1. Assemble the unit by attaching zip ties to connect the corners.
2. Attach the tablecloth by threading wire through it and connecting it to the unit so the color side faces forward.
3. Set the unit up and see how sturdy it is. If it needs reinforcing, try attaching metal rods on the side of the unit and pushing them firmly into the ground.

< Fabric can rot outside, but plastic tablecloths last longer and are easily interchangeable when you are ready for something new.

PLANT FOLIAGE FOR SHADE COLOR

See your shaded areas as an opportunity, not an obstacle

IN GARDEN CENTERS across the nation there can be heard a cry, "I have too much shade and nothing will grow under the trees. I don't know what flowers I can plant!" This problem is readily solved by tossing out the idea of using sun-loving annual flowers entirely and instead trying plants with interesting foliage in a full-shade garden bed.

These part- to full-shade plants make excellent bedding annuals, have colorful or interesting foliage, and will make your garden explode with color.

- Begonia
- Bloodleaf
- Browallia
- Angel wing begonia
- Rex begonia
- Tuberose begonia
- Wax begonia
- Caladium
- Coleus
- Calico plant
- Colocasia
- Creeping Jenny
- Fuchsia
- Lobelia
- New Guinea impatiens
- Polka dog plant
- Sweet potato vine
- Wishbone flower

But shady areas often present special challenges, such as compacted soil, tree roots, and dry conditions.

Annual plants do not like tough ground and tight roots. Often, a difficult shady area beneath a tree or next to a home foundation is filled with compacted soil with dry conditions. Keep this in mind, because you might have to water more often in order to support a shady garden bed. Rain barrel water is perfect for this use, and it's free of heavy chemicals. Soil compaction is when soil density is so thick and pressured that it limits root growth potential and decreases soil drainage. This can be drama for trees, shrubs, perennials, and annual garden beds.

∧ Tropical plants such as alocasia, colocasia, and caladium, while not drought tolerant, are remarkably colorful and versatile. Without a single flower bloom, you can hack a garden bed full of color and delight.

Since most gardeners are unable to remove all the soil in a problem area, the best solution is to amend the soil and layer up. Have your soil tested to see what amendments might be needed. Adding a mixture of compost, rotted manure, and other organic ingredients the first season should help make your planting area more successful. Should you have a lot of trees, it is advisable to consult with an arborist beforehand so you do not harm the root systems in the digging process.

∨ Other fantastic shade to part-shade plants include coleus and sweet potato vine. Here, their bold colors are combined in front of a restaurant window.

∧ Caladium, in particular, come in bold colors such as red, pink, rose, white, chartreuse, and green with lines, spots, and splotches that will dazzle the eye.

93

HACK A FRONT LAWN VEGETABLE GARDEN
A garden CAN be both beautiful and edible

SUPPLIES
NEEDED
- Soil amendments
- Organic fertilizer
- Vegetable plants
- Stakes
- Rope or string
- Hammer
- Shovel or hand trowel
- Mulch

FRONT LAWN VEGETABLE gardens are grown out of need and necessity. No sun in the backyard? Put the veggie garden in the front. Need more garden space? You may have footage out front that is filled with only grass, so using that space is common sense. But designing a front-yard vegetable garden that is attractive and well maintained is particularly important because many cities have regulations regarding front lawn plantings. Thoroughly research your design plan and get the approval of your immediate neighbors, homeowner's association, or city government before you plant.

While others insist on turning their soil over annually, this garden is a till-free, all-organic garden. This means that every year, soil, compost, manure, or mulch are added to the soil, and it is never turned over with a tiller. At the end of the season, simply cut off the tops of the plants, add a 2-inch layer of organic soil or compost or rotted manure, then replant in the spring. No turning or tilling is necessary.

< This front lawn vegetable garden resides in a very traditional suburban neighborhood on the outskirts of Chicago. Annually, the garden produces between 250 and 500 pounds of food for local food pantries.

∧ Creating a design is made easier with hammer, stakes, and string.

HOW TO CREATE A FRONT-LAWN VEGETABLE GARDEN

1. Before planting, amend the soil as needed according to your soil test results (mixing lots of rotted manure and organic matter helps to establish strong roots and is always a healthy idea).
2. Using hammer, stakes, and rope, string your rows out in the sun-ray design.
3. Lay out the plants; make every other row a different variety of plant.
4. Dig a hole for each plant once you are satisfied with the entire layout.
5. Place organic fertilizer in the hole according to package directions and plant.
6. Mulch the area with 2 inches of mulch, being sure not to smother plant stems.
7. Water well.

HACK A TIKI HUT FOR UNDER $100

Even the plainest sheds can clean up nicely with some imagination

TURN AN ORDINARY shed into something extraordinary. Whether made from wood, metal, or plastic resin, with the proper tools and materials, you should be able to create a tiki hut in the garden for under $100 by covering the shed in reed and straw. All the supplies are found at home and garden stores, making this a super-easy do-it-yourself project. Imagine a brand new tiki hut to entertain around with friends—a perfect solution for an ugly shed.

< Using common items found at hardware and home garden centers, you can cover your ugly old resin shed and transform it into a fun tiki hut.

SUPPLIES NEEDED

- Saw
- Drill
- 1½-inch galvanized screws
- Wire cutters
- Scissors
- Industrial stapler or pneumatic staple gun

Measure and estimate your need for:

- Thin strips of 6-foot long wood trim
- Reed fencing (we used 6-foot-high fencing)
- A straw seed-starting mat roll

∧ Install a second layer of wood trim on the sides in order to hold down the straw roofing material.

∧ Add several layers of straw roofing material to make the roof look more natural.

HOW TO HACK A TIKI HUT

1. Use a saw to cut the wood trim pieces that will be placed at the top and the bottom of the shed.
2. Place reed fencing against shed wall.
3. Using galvanized screws, drill trim evenly onto the reed fencing around the bottom and top of the shed, securing it to the wall.
4. Cut extra reed fencing to size with wire cutters at the edge of the building.
5. Place custom measured and cut reed fencing against each of the shed doors. Attach trim onto the reed fencing, securing it to the individual doors.
6. Using wire cutters, cut reeds out of the handle area so you are able to pull the doors open easily without damaging the new covering.
7. Repeat the reed attachment process for the three walls without doors.
8. Your trim should now be holding the reed up to the wall and doors on all sides of the shed.
9. Roll out the straw mat over the roof of the shed until it is covered; let extra mat hang over the sides. You might have to use several layers of matting. We used two layers.
10. Hold mat down with a piece of trim set over the wood you already have drilled into the wall that supports the reed fencing.
11. Drill trim over the existing trim with straw matting between to secure straw mat so the wind will not rip it off of the roof.
12. Staple remnants of matting onto the roof and wood trim to hide the wood trim on the side of the shed from showing.
13. Then trim the "hair" on the roof up with scissors so it looks even.

RECYCLE ART FOR ART'S SAKE
Make your own whimsical artwork for your garden

FOLK ART IS a tradition in the United States. You can make your own folk garden art out of found and reused objects that we would normally throw away. It is the perfect way to contribute to the reuse movement and express yourself creatively.

Be sure that the items you are using are not toxic or chemical-laden as this will defeat your positive environmental action. Keep your garden free of toxic materials whenever possible, and in fact, only paint the items if you feel it is absolutely necessary. In this art creation, chartreuse, purple, red-orange, and blue make a bold color statement.

HOW TO RECYCLE ART

1. Find several large, round, flat items—old wall decorations, wreaths, flattened iron pieces, or flat baskets work perfectly.
2. Spray paint each with bright colors that match your garden's color scheme (or save the paint and leave them as is).
3. Hang on a fence wall as "flower heads" using nails, wire, or staples.
4. Recycle an old electrical cord, hose, or wires to use as the flower's stem and leaves. Staple these onto the fence.
5. Enjoy!

˅ Reused and recycled items getting a new life for wall art with spray paint.

> Recycled garden art looks terrific on fences and shed walls. Try placing your art behind a seating area.

TOOL
hacks

HACKS IN THIS CHAPTER:

LONG-HANDLED TOOL YARDSTICK HACK

The benefits of this hack aren't hard to calibrate

PROPER MEASUREMENTS CAN make all the difference in a garden. Let's say you need to plant seeds 6 inches apart and didn't think to bring out a measuring tape. What if you need to poke holes in the ground 2 inches deep? Or what about the classic bulb dilemma: You have five bags of bulbs and realize that for one bag the bulbs should be planted 4 inches deep and on another bag 12 inches deep. Most gardeners do not carry a measuring tape in their back pocket.

This problem is solved by simply applying a measuring stick on the end of your shovel or other long-handled garden tool. With a permanent marker and a good measuring tape, you can have the problem solved in no time.

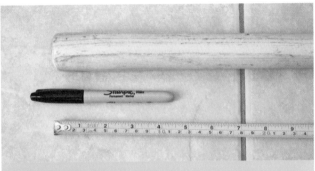

˄ Measuring tape, a permanent marker, and a long-handled gardening tool are all you need to make a convenient garden measuring tool.

SUPPLIES NEEDED	HOW TO MAKE A YARDSTICK
• Measuring tape • Permanent marker • Long-handled gardening tool	1. Place your garden tool on a flat surface. 2. Lay out your tape measure parallel to the tool. 3. Using the tape measure as a guide, use a permanent marker to mark centimeter or inch lines (as needed for your projects) directly onto the handle. Let dry. 4. Measure the world.

< Measuring anything in the garden is easy when you hack a measuring tool directly on to your long-handled gardening equipment.

HOSE KINK PREVENTION HACK
Stop hating hoses with this easy solution

HOSES ARE IMPORTANT to our gardens: Most gardeners need them to care for their plants. Remember that using drinking-water-safe hoses is very important as well, because drinking-water-safe hoses can help deliver a healthier and more organic garden to your family (see Hack 25). Hoses with heavy kinking tendencies can be drama—bendy, heavy, and difficult to move around the garden and patio. Kinky hoses are a source of back pain, particularly for people with physical health conditions. To help prevent injuries and frustration in the garden, it would be best to be rid of the kinks.

Once a kink gets locked in position, it becomes a bend in the hose that frequently re-kinks so that you are faced with constant hose drama. There are solutions, though. You can cut the hose at the kink and placing a threaded insert on each end to help rescue the hose and get rid of the kink. You can also splint the hose: find old hoses and or tubing just a step up in size from the existing hose and thread tightly over the hose and the site of the kink. Lock the splinted portion of the hose tightly with hardware clamps to be sure the splint will hold well.

You can prevent bends and kinks over the life of your hose if you put the hose away in a figure-8 pattern rather than trying to circle the hose around an object or on the ground. Drain the hose of water, then gently bend it (do not force it), and wave the hose into the figure-8 shape for storage.

> When putting your hose away for storage, be sure to gently bend the hose into a figure-8 shape so that the hose is put away without harsh kinks in place.

TWO GOOD REASONS TO TAPE YOUR TOOLS
Mostly, it's to help you find them

TOOLS GET LOST in the garden. We set them down on the ground while weeding or cutting, and they blend in with the mulch and soil because of their wooden handles and natural colors, and are lost. Tools that are left outside get damaged: Handles crack, metal rusts, and colors fade. Keeping your garden tools safe is super-easy with this simple hack—just wrap your tool handles in neon-colored tape. Keep the tape on the handles all the time. They will be much easier to find in the grass, soil, or mulch. And customizing your tools with tape is a great way to identify them as yours if you are working with other people, such as at a community garden.

HOW TO TAPE TOOLS
1. Buy brightly colored tape.
2. Wrap the handles of the tools so they are easier to see.
3. Never lose a tool again.

∧ Hack the tool loss by wrapping their handles with colorful tape. You will never lose a tool in the garden again.

DOOR TOOL HANGER HACK
A handy hack for keeping tools close at hand

THERE'S NEVER ENOUGH room to hang all the tools in the garage or shed, and they are never convenient to grab up at a moment's notice. During garden season, consider a back garage door as a convenient location to store tools.

SUPPLIES NEEDED
- Recycle an old shoe hanger, tie hanger, or purchase a hook meant to hold brooms and cleaning supplies
- Drill
- Screws
- Pencil

HOW TO MAKE A TOOL HANGER
1. Measure the area where you want to install the hanger. Take the length and width of your tools into consideration.
2. Center the hook or strip and measure twice—you want to get this right the first time.
3. Mark holes to drill.
4. Drill holes and insert screws in respective holes.
5. Hang tools.

> Install a tool hanger on a door near the garden, and you will have your tools conveniently on hand whenever you need them. Hanging a photo frame on your tool door is a creative idea—you can leave message for garden helpers or better yet, have an emergency tool stash to defend against zombies.

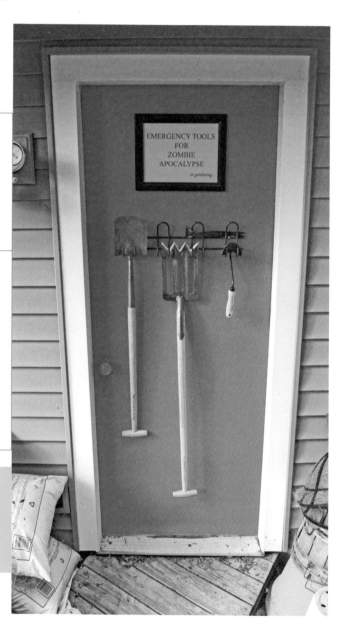

HOW TO WINTERIZE A RAIN BARREL

Prevent your water collection device from bursting

AS THE THERMOMETER plummets, it is time to close up gardens and winterize or weatherize rain barrels. Water that is left to freeze inside a rain barrel will crack and ruin most barrels.

∧ Disconnect the rain barrel and turn it upside down to prevent cracking.

HOW TO WINTERIZE A RAIN BARREL

1. Disconnect rain barrel from downspout.
2. Drain all the water from both the rain barrel and hoses by opening the spigot and allowing the water to drain out completely.
3. Rinse the interior of the barrel to clean out any sediment build up.
4. Let dry.
5. If you are able, relocate your rain barrel into storage or flip the barrel upside down to prevent any water from freezing on the interior of the barrel.
6. Reconnect temporary gutter downspouts to redirect winter roof water away from your home's foundation. Do this by screwing on the downspout you removed in the spring, or by adding temporary flexible down spouting.

∧ Reconnect temporary gutter downspouts to redirect water away from your home's foundation.

< Rain barrels come in all shapes and styles, but care must be taken in the fall in northern zones to prevent water from freezing inside the rain barrel.

101

TURN TOOLS INTO SOMETHING BEAUTIFUL

Trellis garden art made from reused garden tools

OLD GARDEN TOOLS are always laying around the garden; some are ancient, some are rusting, some are broken—but all can be reused. Hang them as a creative trellis on the fence or a back wall instead of throwing them out.

∧ Enjoy beautiful climbing plants on reused and recycled garden tools made into a trellis.

∨ Measure carefully and hang your reused garden tools on a fence and plant a climbing plant below the trellis.

HOW TO MAKE TOOL ART

1. Find a spot on your fence or wall where you would like to create a trellis.
2. Paint the tools (optional).
3. Mark the spots on the tool handles and on the fence or wall where you would like to secure the trellis.
4. Drill holes into the handles that match up with where they should be hung on the fence or wall.
5. Drill the deck screws through the predrilled holes into the fence or wall to build the trellis.
6. Plant a climbing vine below the trellis such a pole beans, cardinal flower, or morning glories, and let the plants twine up around the tools.

SUPPLIES NEEDED

- 3-inch deck screws
- Old shovels, hoes, and rakes
- A drill
- Spray paint (optional)

Dedication & Acknowledgments

I posthumously dedicate this book to my grandmothers.

These fabulous ladies taught me that hard work is a balm for the soul and that sharing your love with another human being is unequivocally the most important thing you can do to make a difference. The world needs more people who teach a small child the power of kindness, sustainability, and sharing as a life lesson.

SPECIAL THANKS to my big, bad, crazy family. My husband and daughters fill every day with an especially good life no matter what hardship we face together. I love you and am thankful for your amazing support.

I am so very grateful for the wonderful team of people who help me create my books. It starts with the terrific staff and editing team at Cool Springs Press—my editor, Mark Johanson, is the best. Steve Roth, Lola Honeybone, and the wonderful marketing team assists me to go out and meet and get to know many of the lovely readers who support my books. Thank you one and all. I could not create a book without a team of passionate awesome-sauce helping me.

There are too many wonderful friends in my life to list on this one page, but I give particular thanks to The Dirty Glove Society, which is a part of my life every day: personal friends who are so deeply entrenched in my heart they are more like family rather than friends.

Special thanks to Ken Druse for his amazing seed-starting formula help. Thank you to Mark Highland of Organic Mechanics Soil for soil and worm casting guidance. Thanks to Annie Haven for her Moo Poo Tea bags and Barbara Sanderson for her bee preserver art. Thanks to Kylee Baumle, Robin Haglund, Andrea Duclos, Patricia Davis, Charles Dowding, Stacy of Olive Loaf Design, Organic Online, Woolly Pockets, and Gardeners.com for their photographic contributions. Also thanks to Eileen Landau, Chicago Botanic Garden, P. Allen Smith, Kylee Baumle, and Pam Penick for allowing me to publish the photos I took of them or their gardens in this book—they are all champion garden hackers.

Conversions

CONVERTING MEASUREMENTS

To Convert:	To:	Multiply by:
Inches	Millimeters	25.4
Inches	Centimeters	2.54
Feet	Meters	0.305
Yards	Meters	0.914
Miles	Kilometers	1.609
Square inches	Square centimeters	6.45
Square feet	Square meters	0.093
Square yards	Square meters	0.836
Cubic inches	Cubic centimeters	16.4
Cubic feet	Cubic meters	0.0283
Cubic yards	Cubic meters	0.765
Pints (US)	Liters	0.473 (Imp. 0.568)
Quarts (US)	Liters	0.946 (Imp. 1.136)
Gallons (US)	Liters	3.785 (Imp. 4.546)
Ounces	Grams	28.4
Pounds	Kilograms	0.454
Tons	Metric tons	0.907

To Convert:	To:	Multiply by:
Millimeters	Inches	0.039
Centimeters	Inches	0.394
Meters	Feet	3.28
Meters	Yards	1.09
Kilometers	Miles	0.621
Square centimeters	Square inches	0.155
Square meters	Square feet	10.8
Square meters	Square yards	1.2
Cubic centimeters	Cubic inches	0.061
Cubic meters	Cubic feet	35.3
Cubic meters	Cubic yards	1.31
Liters	Pints (US)	2.114 (Imp. 1.76)
Liters	Quarts (US)	1.057 (Imp. 0.88)
Liters	Gallons (US)	0.264 (Imp. 0.22)
Grams	Ounces	0.035
Kilograms	Pounds	2.2
Metric tons	Tons	1.1

CONVERTING TEMPERATURES

Degrees Fahrenheit (°F)	Degrees Celsius (°C)
55°	25°
50°	20°
45°	15°
40°	10°
35°	5°
30° — Freezing	0°
25°	-5°
20°	-10°
15°	-15°
10°	-20°
5°	-25°
0°	-30°

METRIC EQUIVALENT

Inches (in.)	$\frac{1}{64}$	$\frac{1}{32}$	$\frac{1}{25}$	$\frac{1}{16}$	$\frac{1}{8}$	$\frac{1}{4}$	$\frac{3}{8}$	$\frac{2}{5}$	$\frac{1}{2}$	$\frac{5}{8}$	$\frac{3}{4}$	$\frac{7}{8}$	1
Feet (ft.)													
Yards (yd.)													
Millimeters (mm)	0.40	0.79	1	1.59	3.18	6.35	9.53	10	12.7	15.9	19.1	22.2	25.4
Centimeters (cm)							0.95	1	1.27	1.59	1.91	2.22	2.54
Meters (m)													

Inches (in.)	2	3	4	5	6	7	8	9	10	11	12	36	39.4
Feet (ft.)											1	3	3½
Yards (yd.)												1	1½
Millimeters (mm)	50.8	76.2	101.6	127	152	178	203	229	254	279	305	914	1,000
Centimeters (cm)	5.08	7.62	10.16	12.7	15.2	17.8	20.3	22.9	25.4	27.9	30.5	91.4	100
Meters (m)											.30	.91	1.00

°F to °C: Subtract 32 from the Fahrenheit temperature reading. Then mulitply that number by $\frac{5}{9}$. For example, 77°F - 32 = 45. 45 × $\frac{5}{9}$ = 25°C.

°C to °F : Multiply the Celsius temperature reading by $\frac{9}{5}$, then add 32. For example, 25°C × $\frac{9}{5}$ = 45. 45 + 32 = 77°F.

Index

Meet Shawna Coronado

Shawna Coronado is a wellness and green living lifestyle advocate. As an author, photographer, and media host, Shawna campaigns globally for social good and health awareness. With a "make a difference" focus on sustainable home living, organic gardening, and healthy food recipes built to inspire, Shawna hopes to stimulate positive changes for her community.

Her garden and eco-adventures have been featured in many media venues including radio and television. Shawna's successful organic living photographs and stories have been shown both online and off in many international home and garden magazines and multiple books. You can meet Shawna by connecting online with her on her blog and website at www.shawnacoronado.com.

Want to read more of Shawna Coronado's organic, green, and ground-breaking books on smart sustainable growing? Find *Grow a Living Wall: Create Vertical Gardens with Purpose* online and at bookstores everywhere.